My Own Cook Book

By Gladys Taber

GLADYS TABER

My Own
Cook Book

From Stillmeadow
and Cape Cod

Drawings by
PAMELA JOHNSON

PARNASSUS IMPRINTS
Orleans, Mass. 02653

For BARBARA LOVELY

With love and appreciation

Contents

Foreword

Cooking is an art that has a great advantage over some of the fine arts we all admire, for its basic tools are available to most of us. With a stove, refrigerator, and a few utensils plus that essential quality all artists possess—imagination—any woman or any man, for that matter, can practice the art of cooking. A stage or a great rehearsal hall or a skylighted studio is not necessary. And all the basic materials are available in supermarkets or the family grocery store.

Cooking has another great advantage in that the family does not have to go far afield to enjoy it. The kitchen is a part of every home, from the smallest city apartment to the most impressive mansion. So the creative outlet of cooking is available to anyone within the four walls of his or her home. And I suspect that no matter what happens in our changing society, the family as a family will survive as long as we do not eat in communal kitchens run by the government.

In our family, we have always found that eating together aids family solidarity. When we face serious personality conflicts or major problems, we have a way of saying, "Well, let's have supper first." We find that tensions ease and difficulties can be handled after we have gathered around the table and had a good meal.

In fact, I believe that family life began when that first primitive man discovered that digging a hole and heating some rocks and tossing in the raw game meant that everyone then sat around in a circle

11

to consume the charred meats and fowl. Much later, someone tossed grain in the hole and poured water in, and a mush resulted. This was, I feel, the beginning of civilization. From this undoubtedly came the idea of every man contributing a share and everyone sharing what he had brought.

From this beginning evolved the lavish eras when kings and queens gave banquets to reflect their status. More attention was paid, I think, to how many courses were served than to how many jewels the women wore.

When we come to the beginning of our own country, we read about the first Thanksgiving of the Pilgrims; as one who has often had unexpected guests, I can sympathize with the Pilgrim Fathers who suddenly had ninety or so Indians descending to join the feast. In this instance, the guests had to go out and bring in some extras, which were nineteen deer as I recall the story. The party lasted several days until the rum ran out, but it was very successful. Wild turkeys, corn, squash, deer, and rum made a satisfactory menu.

In our present society, I notice that eating together still has a profound meaning. Heads of governments are entertained at dinners. National decisions are made over breakfasts, and although we may never be told about the decisions reached, we always hear about the omelets and sautéed chicken livers, etc., that were served. In fact, much of our life seems to revolve around people eating together, even to the endless chicken à la king and peas served at campaign rallies.

I am heartily in favor of this custom, since I feel that when we eat together, we tend to be more amiable about taxes, wars, the economy, and so on.

As far as cooking itself goes, I have always loved to cook. I have a few friends who say they simply hate cooking, but nonetheless most of them like to eat a really delicious meal and are an appreciative audience for those like myself who practice the art of cooking! It is true there is a lot of drudgery in cooking; I do not like to scrape carrots, peel onions, or mince things. And I think separating eggs is a bore. But I cannot think of anything in the world that does not involve some uninteresting chores. Ballet dancers spend hours practicing at those bars. Painters work away cleaning brushes and mixing colors, and musicians toil all day going over one passage in a symphony.

Actors practice incessantly, too. People in business spend a good deal of time going over reports. Lawyers work on tedious briefs. Doctors spend time on mundane things—taking temperatures and reading X-rays—television's Marcus Welby to the contrary.

But cooking has one great advantage over the other arts. While you are doing the mechanical part of it, you can think about anything in the world! I often recite my favorite poetry or sing to myself or remember happy moments. If I have to wait for something to simmer, I have a book handy to dip into. The mind can range over the wide horizon while you beat egg whites for a soufflé!

Finally, I think one reason that some women hate to cook is that they work in a sterile atmosphere. The smallest kitchen can have charm if you decide to give it some. One friend of mine with a dreadful old refrigerator painted the front with swirls of sea blue. Another Scotch-taped colorful cutouts from magazines on dingy walls. Another kept plants blooming on the windowsill. Another decorated the cupboard doors with Hawaiian surf advertisements. One of the most charming kitchens I know belongs to Eileen DeLory on Cape Cod. Copper and cast-iron and wooden utensils hang on hooks all over the room and catch the sunlight coming in over the water. Bunches of drying herbs and sweet red onions hang over the counters.

The working equipment a cook uses depends on her own personality. I find it is a good idea to sit down and list what you like best to use and then pack away all the extras. A cluttered kitchen is hard to work in and hard to take care of. I filled a shelf in the guest-room closet at Still Cove with casseroles, skillets, roasting pans, salad bowls, and cake tins. They are available in case of emergency, and now I have more space in the kitchen. At Stillmeadow, there is a large back kitchen where we keep the big soup kettle, the Dutch oven, the chafing dish, the fondue cooker, and the waffle iron.

Arranging the equipment involves putting utensils as near as possible to where you use them. For instance, at one time I kept my electric toaster in the corner of the counter across the room from the breadbox and the refrigerator where the butter was. One day I moved the toaster to the counter near the bread and butter, and what a difference! I also discovered that keeping a glass apothecary jar of flour beside the range made thickening sauces easy. And I now have seasoned salt and pepper in three places, over the range on the herb shelf, over the counter where I mix salad, and on the table by the window.

The recipes in this book are chosen from my personal collection, most of them the favorite recipes of many friends who have been good enough to share them. Half the fun of discovering a new recipe is to share it. I have also repeated a few that are most often requested by readers of my books and columns. I am always happy when someone writes me to say that her husband keeps suggesting they have Gladys Taber's Pork Chops and Cabbage for dinner. The few friends I have who enjoy keeping their recipes secret miss a lot!

I choose for my own kitchen recipes that are for the most part not too time-consuming. I have a good many gourmet cookbooks, and I love to read them and imagine what it would be like to spend all day on one dish with truffles and wine and so on. But most of us in these busy times simply cannot spend hours on a magnificent production! Occasionally at Stillmeadow, on a holiday, I cook up something that takes hours of tender care, but actually any simple meal, well cooked and seasoned with imagination, makes dining a pleasure.

For the most part I have collected recipes that do not call for ingredients that many of us cannot buy. In big cities there are special shops where you may buy exotic imported products, but the supermarket or the country store supplies the needs of the majority of kitchens in our country. And I am always amazed at how successfully they do so.

I hope these cherished recipes from Stillmeadow and Still Cove will bring happy cooking!

G. T.

My Own
Cook Book

APPETIZERS

ASPARAGUS ROLL-UPS

Remove crusts from thin slices of bread. Spread each slice with soft butter and mayonnaise. Sprinkle chopped chives over each slice. Place an asparagus tip on each. (For cooking asparagus properly, see "Vegetables.") Roll the bread up around the tips and wrap in waxed paper.

When ready to serve, run under the broiler until the bread is toasted and the asparagus heated. Serve at once on a warm plate.

DRIED BEEF CANAPÉS

Use thin slices of dried beef and spread with cream cheese seasoned with prepared mustard (use Dijon mustard, if possible). Roll up carefully and tightly and fasten with cocktail picks.

If you are very deft, you can make cornucopias out of the roll-ups. If you do this, tuck one bit of parsley in the top of the cornucopia.

CANAPÉS SPECIAL

 1   8-oz pkg cream cheese
 1   egg yolk
   Grated onion to taste (start with 1 tsp)
   Paprika
   Dash of seasoned salt
   Crackers

Blend all ingredients well—except the crackers. Spread mixture on crackers and broil until puffed up and golden.

MAKES 12 or more, depending on the size of the crackers you use.

Most guests will eat at least five!

CHEESE HOOIES

 ¼   lb strong cheese
 ¼   lb butter
 1   tsp seasoned salt
   Dash of cayenne pepper
 1   cup sifted flour
   Powdered sugar

Grate the cheese into the butter and cream well. Add salt and cayenne pepper. Work the flour in until blended, then knead on a board until smooth. Roll into a long thin roll. Chill. Slice thinly. Bake on a cookie sheet at 350° until beginning to brown (8 minutes or more). Dust with powdered sugar.

Double this recipe for a party.

MAKES 12–15, depending on how thin your roll is.

I am repeating this recipe because I get a good many letters asking for it. It is a standby for appetizers or just for nibbling any time. Cheese Hooies keep better than almost any other type of cocktail tidbits. I discovered them when I lived in Virginia. I have no idea why they are called Hooies, and the hostess who first served them to me had no idea either. She said they had always been called Hooies.

DE LUXE CHEESE SPREAD

½ lb sharp Cheddar cheese
½ lb blue cheese
½ lb Port Salut cheese
½ lb butter
½ lb cream cheese
2 cups commercial sour cream

Seasoned salt to taste
Worcestershire sauce (about 1 tsp)
Tabasco (try a few drops and taste)
¼–½ tsp garlic, crushed

Put the first 5 ingredients through a food chopper. Add sour cream and seasonings. Beat with electric beater until soft.

Use as a spread or dip with Melba toast or unsalted crackers.

SERVES 12–15

This keeps well in the refrigerator, but let it come to room temperature when you serve it. If you are lucky enough to have small stoneware crocks, serve it in them. I don't, so I use those white French ramekins. Looks pretty too!

INEZ PARKINS'S CHRISTMAS CHEESE BALL

½ lb natural Cheddar, grated
1   3-oz pkg cream cheese
3   tbsp sherry
¼ cup chopped, pitted olives
½ tsp Worcestershire sauce
    Dash each of garlic and onion salt
½ cup chopped dried beef

Several days ahead beat the cheeses with the sherry, olives, Worcester-shire sauce and salts until thoroughly combined. Shape into a ball and wrap in foil. Refrigerate at least overnight. About 30 minutes before serving, remove foil and roll the cheese ball in the dried beef.

SERVES 10–15

This is a delightful appetizer for Christmas. You may also roll it in chopped parsley to lend a green touch for Twelfth Night.

HOT CLAM CANAPÉS

1   3-oz pkg cream cheese
2   tbsp heavy cream
1   cup minced clams
1   tbsp Worcestershire sauce
    Dash of dry mustard
    Dash of seasoned salt
½ tsp grated onion

Combine all ingredients and pile lightly on small toast triangles or rounds. Broil until the canapés puff up.

MAKES 12–15

A hot canapé is always welcome along with cold dips and spreads. This is easy and a favorite either with cocktails or as hors d'oeuvres.

CHAFING-DISH CLAM DIP

1   small onion, finely chopped
½   green pepper, diced
3   tbsp butter
1   10½-oz can minced clams
¼   lb process cheese, cut in strips
4   tbsp catsup
1   tbsp Worcestershire sauce
1   tbsp sherry
¼   tsp cayenne pepper

Sauté the onion and pepper in butter for 3 minutes, then add the remaining ingredients and cook until the cheese melts, stirring constantly. Keep it hot in the blazer of the chafing dish with the bottom container partly filled with simmering water. If you have no chafing dish you may use an earthenware casserole over a candle warmer. It must be kept hot.

Serve with crisp crackers or Melba toast.

SERVES 6–12

SEA-SONG CLAM PUFFS

¼ cup butter, melted
1   3-oz pkg cream cheese
2   cans minced clams, drained
1   tsp Worcestershire sauce
    Spice Islands Beau Monde, Fines Herbes,
        Sweet Basil, Spices Parisienne to taste
    Lemon–pepper seasoning
24 small squares of bread

Combine melted butter and cheese and stir until blended. Add remaining ingredients except the bread. Toast the bread pieces on one side, then pile on the mixture. Arrange on a cookie sheet and place under the broiler until puffy.

MAKES 24

I first had this elegant appetizer at the Kruzons' on Freeman Lane on Cape Cod. Margaret Kruzon says if you haven't Spice Islands herbs, you may use whatever seasonings you have, and you may vary them as you wish. The delicate puffs (and they do puff) come from the server golden brown.

SEA-SONG SALAMI ROLLS

With the puffs, Margaret served rolled-up slices of thin salami stuffed with cream cheese, and a big tray of crisp vegetables for nibbling.

BLUE CHEESE SPREAD

¼ lb blue cheese
1 3-oz pkg cream cheese
3 tbsp soft butter
1 tsp paprika
1 tsp Worcestershire sauce

Cream the blue cheese with the back of a spoon, add the cream cheese and butter. Beat well with a spoon. Add seasonings and blend together.

SERVES 6

This is always popular for a cocktail spread and can be made ahead.

KAY'S CHUTNEY SPREAD

1 8-oz pkg cream cheese
½ cup chutney
½ tsp curry powder
¼ tsp dry mustard

Drain the chutney and chop it fine if necessary, then add the softened cheese. Add curry and mustard and mix well. Use crisp crackers for spreading.

SERVES 6–12

Kay, my Cape Cod neighbor at Tickitock Hill, makes her own chutney, and oh, how delicious! It is a secret recipe from Scotland. For the nearest I can come to it, see Green Tomato Chutney in "Pickles and Preserves."

Kay often has guests for afternoon tea, and the neighborhood women gather to watch the sailing boats on Mill Pond while their husbands are off fishing.

STUFFED EGGS WITH MUSHROOMS

6 large mushrooms
1 shallot or small green onion
1 tsp chopped parsley
6 hard-cooked eggs
1 tbsp butter
   Seasoned salt and pepper
1 tbsp wine or cream
   Seasoned or plain bread crumbs

Chop the mushrooms with the shallot or onion and parsley. Cut the eggs in half, remove the yolks, and mix with mushrooms and onion. Melt the butter in a skillet and add mushroom mixture and seasonings. Moisten with wine or cream and cook 5 or 10 minutes over low heat, just until the mushrooms are tender. Stuff the egg whites with this mixture, sprinkle the crumbs on top, dot with butter, arrange on toast rounds, and broil until the crumbs brown.

SERVES 4–6

You may serve these chilled for hors d'oeuvres or hot for a buffet dish. If you cannot get fresh mushrooms, use the best large canned ones, but the fresh are better.

GUACAMOLE

1 avocado
1 clove garlic
1 small hot pepper
1 tbsp coriander leaves (or parsley)
  Seasoned salt
  Juice of ½ lime

Mash the avocado with a fork. Chop the garlic, pepper (seeded) and coriander or parsley together. Add to the avocado with the salt and lime juice. Serve in a bowl as a dip.

For a party dip, plan on 1 avocado to 2 persons. If you make the dip ahead, spread a thin layer of mayonnaise over the top to keep it from turning dark. Chill. Then mix the mayonnaise in just before serving. Use whatever you want for dipping. We like corn chips.

MARINATED MUSHROOMS

1   lb mushrooms, cut lengthwise with stem on
¼ cup chopped parsley
2   cloves garlic, minced
½ tsp seasoned salt
½ tsp seasoned pepper
½ cup olive oil
3   tbsp wine vinegar

Combine ingredients in a crockery or Pyrex bowl. Refrigerate for a couple of hours. Keep the bowl covered.

Serve with tiny canapé forks or toothpicks.

SERVES 6–8, normally.

Four dedicated mushroom eaters will nibble until the bowl is empty!

HELENE'S PARTY SPECIAL

1   cup melted currant jelly
½   cup spicy mustard (the hotter the better)
2   12-oz pkg miniature frankfurters

Mix the jelly and mustard well and put into a large casserole. Add the frankfurters and bake 30 minutes in a 350° oven.

Serve hot with toothpicks for spearing.

SERVES 6

This gives a lift to the usual cheese and crackers and nuts for a cocktail party. If you have a chafing dish, you can serve from it, keeping the heat very low. My chafing dish is an old-fashioned copper one and burns liquid fuel. Almost shutting the cover of the burning unit helps to keep the heat low enough.

BUBBLY ONION CANAPÉS

3   tbsp finely chopped onion
3   tbsp mayonnaise
    Seasoned salt and pepper
2   drops Tabasco
½   tsp paprika

Mix all ingredients together and spread on crackers. Broil under low heat until the mixture bubbles. Be sure to cover the crackers completely so the edges will not burn.

MAKES 10–12

RUTH WALKER'S LIVER MOLD

1 can condensed consommé
1 envelope Knox gelatin
    Chopped parsley and chives to taste
8 oz whipped cream cheese
1 can liver spread
1 tsp lemon juice

Bring the soup to a boil and dissolve the gelatin in it. Add herbs and let cool. Mix cheese, liver and lemon juice. Oil a bowl or mold and put some of the cooled soup in the bottom. When this sets, put the cheese mixture in, then top with remaining soup. Chill in refrigerator until set. Serve on a small platter surrounded by crisp crackers. Cut in slices with a small knife, and let the guests serve themselves as often as they wish.

SERVES 6

I first had this at Ruth and Charlotte's house, the Bowed Roof, overlooking the ocean on Cape Cod. Charlotte's cocktails and happy conversation added to the evening. I won't admit how much of the appetizer I ate!

SARDINE SPREAD

1   can sardines
1   3-oz pkg creamed cheese
⅛   tsp prepared horseradish
1   tsp minced onion
   Seasoned salt and pepper to taste

Pour the oil off the sardines and mash them well. Blend in the cream cheese and add remaining ingredients.

SERVES 4–6

If you feel as I do about sardines, you will enjoy this. I find just plain sardines, even with a dash of lemon juice, a little too rich for my taste. But this is a fine spread, especially if you are lucky enough to have imported sardines.

CRAB MEAT SALAD ROLLS

Frankfurter rolls
Crab meat salad

Split the rolls and scrape out some of the soft center. Spread on the salad and put the rolls together again. Wrap in foil or waxed paper and chill thoroughly. Cut in 1″ pieces for serving.

SERVES 4–6

This is lovely on a hot summer day with cool drinks.

AMITY HILL SHRIMP

1   lb shrimp (cooked and deveined)
½   lb bacon (thin slices as possible)
1   cup chili sauce
1   clove garlic, minced
½   tsp Beau Monde
½   tsp sugar
    Dash of Worcestershire sauce
    Splash of sherry or white cooking wine

Mix all ingredients except the shrimp a few hours ahead. Then dip each shrimp in the sauce, wrap in ½ slice of bacon, secure with toothpick. (At this point you may refrigerate to hold.) When you are ready to serve, broil shrimp until bacon is crisp.

Serve in chafing dish or electric skillet with the rest of the sauce.

SERVES 6–8

I first tasted this wonderful appetizer at Gail Rainey and Jan Kruzon's house on the hill on Cape Cod. The house is charming and well furnished with various animals, as a house should be, but the guests did not leave one solitary shrimp for the four-footed occupants!

Gail and Jan lead busy lives, Gail in her medical laboratory and Jan as a teacher, but on occasional days off they take time to dig clams, hunt for driftwood and entertain the neighbors.

PIQUANT SAUCE

4 egg yolks
5 tsp prepared mustard
1 tsp seasoned salt
3 tbsp dried dill or ½ cup minced fresh dill
½ tsp seasoned pepper
1 cup chilled olive oil
2 tbsp white vinegar (or use wine vinegar)

Beat first 6 ingredients thoroughly with electric beater (or a hand one). Add oil, 1 teaspoon at a time, continuing to beat. Then beat in vinegar slowly.

Serve with raw vegetables, cherry tomatoes or cleaned, cooked shrimp.

MAKES 1½ cups

Sometimes I think there are so many variations of dips and sauces that I might, one day, just throw in everything I have and beat it and see what happens! But this recipe is especially good when followed exactly.

FELIPE'S SAUCE

2   No. 2 (16-oz) cans tomatoes
¼   tsp garlic powder
1   red chili pepper, crushed
     Pinch of cumin
½   small onion, chopped fine
3   green Tabasco peppers, chopped fine
1   or 2 Jalapeño peppers, chopped fine

Mash tomatoes and mix with the remaining ingredients in a blender. Put in refrigerator to chill. Serve with potato chips or corn chips or whatever for spreading and dipping.

SERVES 6–8

I admit I never have cumin or Jalapeño peppers. But this is still a fine dip. It came from Lola, my California friend, and is a standby at her house.

MABEL'S CURRIED ALMONDS

2 cups whole blanched almonds
1 tbsp butter
2 tsp seasoned salt
¾ tsp curry powder

Spread the nuts in a shallow baking pan. Dot with butter. Bake in a 350° oven about 20 minutes or until golden and toasty brown. When butter melts, stir the nuts or shake the pan to coat the nuts evenly. Remove from oven. Blend seasoned salt and curry powder with a mortar and pestle and sprinkle over nuts. Stir thoroughly. Return to the oven for a few minutes so the seasonings will bake in. Remove from oven and spread on absorbent paper to cool.

MAKES 2 cups.

Mabel Sherrill made these for her own wedding party when she married Lloyd Southworth. They were favorites with every guest. Mabel says you may curry unroasted cashews the same way and they are just as delicious!

FRANCES'S SUGARED NUTS

½ cup brown sugar
¼ cup white sugar
¼ cup sour cream
3   cups whole mixed nuts

Combine sugars and cream and stir over medium heat until dissolved. Boil to soft-ball stage (238° if you have a candy thermometer; otherwise drop a bit in cold water—it forms a soft ball when done). Remove from heat, add nuts, and stir until the mixture sugars. Pour carefully onto waxed paper and separate the nuts with a spoon.

MAKES 4 cups.

Around holiday time you may get tired of the same salted or dry-roasted nuts, good as they are. These sugared nuts add a graceful note, especially if you happen to have a small silver bowl to hold them!

SOUPS

CREAM OF ASPARAGUS SOUP

1	lb asparagus or 1 package frozen asparagus stalks
1	slice lemon
1½	cups chicken consommé
2	tbsp butter
2	tbsp flour
3	cups heated milk and cream
	Seasoned salt and pepper to taste

Cook the asparagus and drain, saving the liquid. Remove the tips. Add stalks and lemon to the chicken consommé and cook about 5 minutes, then purée in your blender, or force through a sieve. Melt butter, blend in flour until smooth. Add the strained soup and cook gently about 5 minutes. Add the milk and cream and seasonings. Place the asparagus tips in heated soup plates and pour the soup over.

SERVES 6

When asparagus is in season and you have served it in all the ways you can think of, this recipe is a friend in need.

BAKED BEAN SOUP

1 medium-sized onion	2 sprigs parsley
1 clove garlic	1 bay leaf
1 green pepper	Seasoned salt and pepper
1 tbsp bacon fat	1 large can baked beans without
1 cup chopped fresh tomatoes	tomato sauce
2 cups consommé	1 tsp red wine
1 stalk celery, diced	Lemon slices

Sauté the onion, garlic, and green pepper in bacon fat until tender. Then add the tomatoes, consommé, celery, parsley, bay leaf, and seasonings. Add the beans and simmer about 30 minutes, then put through a sieve (or use your blender), reheat, and add the wine just before serving. Serve in heated bowls with lemon slices on top.

SERVES 4–6

Serve this with a tossed salad and plenty of coffee.

CHEDDAR SOUP

1 tbsp butter
1 tbsp finely chopped onion
1 tbsp flour
1 cup chicken stock or consommé
2 cups top milk
¾ cup grated Cheddar cheese

Melt the butter, add onion, and cook until golden. Blend in the flour, then add the chicken stock and milk, stirring constantly. Bring just to boiling, add cheese, and stir until the cheese is melted. Garnish with chopped parsley or chives.

SERVES 6

It never serves 6 at Stillmeadow because we like a whole supper of it with a big salad and hot corn bread. Coffee and, for dessert, only fruit.

BLENDER COUNTRY SOUP

1 large can whole tomatoes (or an equal amount
    fresh from the garden)
1 small onion
2 carrots
2 stalks celery
1 green pepper
2 bouillon cubes

Put tomatoes in the blender. Cut the vegetables in pieces and add, then add the bouillon cubes and enough water to fill the container within an inch of the top. Blend on high speed until the vegetables are chopped. Pour soup into a kettle and simmer about 25 minutes.

SERVES 4

This is a fine soup for unexpected guests because you will probably have most of the ingredients right at hand. I use canned beef bouillon if I have it.

OLD DROVER'S INN CHEESE SOUP

4   tbsp butter
½   cup each diced carrot, green pepper, and celery
½   cup minced onion
⅓   cup flour
1   qt chicken stock, or canned chicken bouillon, or chicken
     bouillon cubes dissolved in boiling water
6   oz mild Cheddar cheese, grated
6   oz sharp Cheddar, grated
3   or 4 cups top milk
    Salt and white pepper to taste

Melt butter in the top of a double boiler. Add vegetables and braise until tender. Blend in flour and cook 1 minute, stirring constantly. Add stock and cook until thickened, stirring. (If you use chicken stock, season it before adding.) Now place over boiling water in the top of a double boiler, add cheeses, and cook until they melt. Add milk to thin the mixture until it is creamy and smooth. Season with salt and pepper. Strain. Reheat in the double boiler. Serve hot.

MAKES 2 quarts

This soup may also be chilled and served cold on a hot day.

ICED CHICKEN CURRY SOUP

Butter
2 medium-sized tart apples, peeled, cored, sliced thin
2 medium-sized onions, sliced
1 tsp flour
2 tsp curry powder
Seasoned salt and pepper to taste
Dash of cayenne pepper
1 pint chicken consommé
½ pint dry white wine
½ cup diced cooked chicken
1 cup light cream, chilled

Melt enough butter in a heavy saucepan to sauté the apples and onions gently. Do not let them brown. Blend and add the flour and curry powder, and cook 5 minutes more. Add the seasonings, consommé, and wine, and simmer about 10 minutes, stirring constantly. Remove from heat and strain through a sieve, or use your blender. Cool, then chill in the refrigerator. When ready to serve, add the chicken and the cream. Serve in chilled soup cups.

SERVES 4

This was originally supposed to be a Senegalese soup, but it tastes delicious on a hot August day in New England.

CREAM OF CUCUMBER SOUP

1½   lbs cucumbers (or 3 medium cucumbers)
½   cup minced shallots, scallions, or onions
3   tbsp butter
6   cups chicken broth (your own chicken stock
       or canned broth and water)
1½   tsp wine vinegar
¾   tsp dried dill or tarragon
4   tbsp quick-cooking Cream of Wheat (farina)
       Seasoned salt and pepper to taste
½   cup sour cream

Peel the cucumbers and cut into very thin slices until you have 18 or 20 slices. Cut the remaining cucumbers into ½″ chunks (you need around 4½ cups). Cook shallots, onions, and scallions in butter until tender but not brown. Add the cucumber chunks, chicken broth, vinegar, and herbs. Bring to a boil and stir in the farina. Simmer, partly covered, for 20 to 25 minutes. Purée this mixture and return to the pan. Season. Just before serving beat in sour cream. (Or, if you are worried about calories, use half milk and half cream.) Serve cold garnished with cucumber slices and a light drift of freeze-dried chives. Or put a bit of fresh parsley in each bowl.

SERVES 4–6

We like it as a main dish for a hot summer night with a fresh vegetable salad laced with thin slivers of ham. Thin slices of very dark bread with sweet butter add the perfect touch. Dessert can be Vermont country cheese and crackers.

NEW ENGLAND CLAM CHOWDER

2 dozen hard-shell clams in the shell
¼ lb salt pork
1 onion, minced
3 tbsp flour
2 cups diced raw potatoes
3 tbsp butter
4 cups top milk
   Parsley, seasoned salt, paprika, a pinch of thyme

Scrub the clams well with a firm brush. Put in a deep kettle and pour over 1 cup of water. Steam, tightly covered, until the shells open. Remove clam meats and chop the hard portions. Strain the juice through cheesecloth and add 2 cups of water. Dice the salt pork and sauté over low heat until crisp and golden. Add onion and cook until transparent, then add hard part of the clams. Cook slowly for 5 minutes. Sprinkle the flour over and add clam juice and water, then add potatoes, cover, and simmer until the potatoes are tender but not mushy. Add the soft part of the clams and the butter, and when the chowder comes to a boil, add the milk, heated but not boiling. Add seasonings. Let the chowder ripen at least half an hour. Reheat, but do not boil. Serve hot with toasted chowder crackers.

SERVES 6

You may use 2 cans of minced clams if you have to. I also use part light cream instead of all milk. And I use more salt pork. Serve in warm bowls with extra butter floating on top.

NEW ENGLAND FISH CHOWDER

¼   lb salt pork
½   cup diced onion
2   lbs haddock, cod, or almost any good fish
     Seasoned salt and pepper to taste
½   bay leaf
⅛   tsp thyme
4   potatoes, peeled and diced
1½ qts half milk, half light cream

Remove rind from salt pork and dice the pork. Sauté in a heavy kettle, slowly, until crisp and brown. Remove and in the fat cook the onions until golden. Sprinkle fish with salt and pepper, cover with water, add bay leaf and thyme, and simmer about 30 minutes, or until fish flakes easily. Lift fish out and remove skin and bones. Break the fish in small pieces. Strain the stock and add to salt pork and onions. Cook the potatoes in the stock until tender but not mushy. Add the fish, milk, and salt pork. Season and heat, but do not boil. Serve hot with chowder crackers.

SERVES 6

On Cape Cod, during the fishing season, flounder and bass or bluefish may go into the chowder, and a few pieces of lobster meat add elegance. Serve with toasted chowder crackers and a tossed salad.

FISH CHOWDER DELUXE

¼ lb salt pork, diced
4   medium-sized onions, diced
4   medium-sized potatoes, peeled
    and diced
4   lbs haddock, flounder, or white-
    fish—the more kinds the
    better, except mackerel,
    which is too oily
4   tbsp butter
½   cup flour

3   tsp seasoned salt
½   tsp seasoned pepper
½   tsp sugar
¼   tsp thyme
1   tbsp parsley flakes
    Dash of cayenne pepper
1   qt milk
1   cup light cream
    Paprika

Fry the salt pork in a heavy kettle until crisp (use low heat). Remove salt pork and add onions to the fat and cook until tender, then add potatoes and enough water to cover them. Cook, covered, over moderate heat until potatoes are just tender but not soggy. Rinse the fish and cut crosswise in fairly large pieces. In another kettle or saucepan simmer the fish in just enough water to cover for about 15 minutes, or until it flakes easily. Strain the stock into the potato and onion mixture. Take all bones and skin from the fish and add to the first kettle. Now melt the butter in a Dutch oven or kettle and blend in the flour and seasonings. Slowly add milk and cream, stirring until thickened and smooth. Add the fish mixture and simmer for about 15 minutes, covered. Cool and store in the refrigerator overnight.

Before serving, heat gently, stirring constantly. Do not boil, as boiling will toughen the fish. If the chowder is too thick, add some more cream while it is heating. Sprinkle with paprika and serve in deep bowls with crackers.

MAKES 4 quarts

This is a favorite on Cape Cod when the man in the house brings home a good catch of fish. After you have it baked, fried, broiled, and in fish cakes, you can create a fish chowder and freeze it.

This is a meal in one, but you may serve a tossed salad with it if you feel in the mood.

SCALLOP STEW

1 lb bay scallops
3 cups milk or half milk and half light cream,
    or 1 cup evaporated milk and 2 cups milk
2 tbsp butter or more

Place scallops in a heavy kettle and add enough water to barely cover (about an inch). Heat for five minutes, but do not let come to a boil. Add milk and heat but do not boil. Pour into a heated soup tureen and top with the butter. Serve in heated soup bowls.

SERVES 4

Jimmy and Eileen DeLory, Cape Cod friends of mine, hunt their own scallops. When I go over to their charming waterfront house for scallop stew, Jimmy always points out it is a free meal, gift from the sea. However, to hunt scallops they have to wear heavy waders that may cost as much as fifty dollars and wade up to the waist in icy water, which reminds me of the old saying that you do not get something for nothing!

Eileen serves raw spinach salad and coffee with the stew and for dessert fresh ripe pears sliced in quarters. She says she prefers using the evaporated milk (see above) as it gives a creamier texture. She uses no salt; the scallops provide that.

CREAM OF CRAB SOUP

2 hard-cooked eggs
3 tbsp butter
Rind of 1 lemon, grated
1 tbsp flour
1 tsp Worcestershire sauce
2 cups fresh crab meat (or frozen
    if necessary)

4 or 5 fresh mushrooms, chopped
2 stalks celery, minced
1 shallot or green onion, minced
4 cups top milk
1 cup cream
Seasoned salt and pepper
1 cup dry sherry

Blend the eggs, butter, lemon rind, flour, and Worcestershire sauce into a smooth paste and mix with the crab meat. Now sauté the mushrooms, celery, and onion in butter for about 5 minutes or so. Place the milk in a double boiler and let it become scalding, add the cream, then the crab meat and egg mixture and the remaining ingredients and seasonings. Let the soup thicken and just before serving, add the sherry. Serve in heated bowls.

SERVES 4–6

Canned crab meat may be used as a substitute if you have no fresh or frozen.

LOBSTER BISQUE

2	medium-sized cooked lob-sters	8	peppercorns
2½	cups chicken consommé	¼	cup butter
1	onion, sliced	¼	cup flour
3	celery ribs with tops	3	cups milk
1	bay leaf	1	cup hot cream
2	whole cloves	1	tbsp dry sherry, if desired

Remove lobster meat and dice. Crush the shells and add them with the ends of the claws to the chicken consommé, onion, celery, bay leaf, cloves, and peppercorns. Simmer for ½ hour, then strain. Melt butter, blend in flour, and add the milk gradually. When smooth and bubbling, add the lobster and stock and simmer, covered, about 5 minutes. Stir in the cream and sherry, and serve in warm bowls.

MAKES 6 servings

If you have the lobster coral, mash it and blend into the butter, then add flour and pour the milk (heated) over.

CAPE COD OYSTER STEW

1   qt oysters with their liquor
½   cup butter
3   cups hot milk
1   cup hot cream
     Seasoned salt and pepper to taste
     Paprika

Heat the oysters in a heavy kettle just until the edges begin to curl, adding the butter as they begin to heat. Add milk and cream and seasonings. Turn the heat off as the milk and cream are added. When the oysters begin to rise in the stew, serve at once in heated bowls with paprika on top.

SERVES 4

I once gave a number of Cape recipes to a magazine and had an irate letter from a reader who told me paprika was entirely wrong for chowder, etc. But I think it looks pretty, so I use it.

OYSTER BISQUE

1   pint oysters with their liquor
2   tbsp butter
2   tbsp flour
2½   cups milk
¾   cup cream

Heat the oysters until the edges curl, remove and chop them. Melt the butter in a heavy kettle, blend in the flour, cook until smooth. Add oyster liquor, milk, and cream, and just bring to a boil. Add oysters and remove from fire.

SERVES 2–4

If you like a creamy soup, this will be your choice.

GOLDEN LENTIL SOUP

1   package lentils
½   stick butter
2   large onions, finely chopped
3   stalks celery, finely chopped
1   medium potato, finely diced
1   large carrot, finely chopped
4   qts chicken stock (or chicken broth,
        preferably College Inn)
    Salt and pepper to taste

Soak the lentils in warm water for 2 hours. Skin the lentils by gently rubbing them between your palms under slightly running water. The skins will rise to the top and can be removed with cupped hands.

Melt butter in a large kettle and add onion and celery. When golden, add remaining ingredients, including the drained lentils. Bring to a boil, then simmer for 1 hour. Add salt and pepper.

MAKES 6 quarts

This recipe is from John Schwalbe, my favorite innkeeper. John was born in Aachen, Germany, and the family moved to America when he was ten years old. His charming, gentle wife, Marie, was born in New York City, of German parents. John and Marie now live in an enchanting ancient house, full of treasures, not the least of which is their gay small poodle who is always the first to welcome us. Dinner with John and Marie is like visiting a fairyland. It is what my granddaughter Anne calls a "happening," which is her highest praise. When Barbara and Slim Lovely and I feel the world has been far too much with us, we drive along a sunset road to enjoy the warm hospitality at the Inn of the Golden Ox, the good conversation, and a never-to-be-forgotten dinner. We often tell John we would like lentil soup for the whole meal!

LENTIL SOUP SUPREME

¼	cup diced onions
½	cup diced celery
½	cup diced carrots
¼	lb raw bacon, diced
½	cup chopped leeks
1	cup cooked lentils
2	tbsp tomato paste
1½	cups bouillon
	Salt and pepper to taste
1	tbsp vinegar
4	frankfurters, sliced thin and sautéed in butter

Mix together all ingredients except the vinegar and frankfurters, and cook about 45 minutes. Cool slightly, then put in the blender and blend until smooth. Add vinegar and frankfurters and bring to a boil.

SERVES 4–6

This recipe was given to me by a wonderful German chef named Wolfgang. I wrote it down on the back of a correspondence card I had in my purse and did my best to translate it afterwards. The first time I tried it I used raw, dried lentils but decided it is better to precook them after soaking all night, as lentils have a mind of their own. This soup is so good you do not want to have the rest of the dinner, just more soup!

JILL'S SPLIT PEA SOUP

2 cups dried peas or lentils
2 sliced potatoes
2 sliced onions
 Pinch of mixed herbs
 Salt and pepper to taste
 Ham bone or veal knuckle or soup bones (ham is best)

Soak the peas overnight. In the morning, drain, cover with fresh water, add the potatoes, onions, herbs, salt, and pepper. Add the bones and simmer several hours. Remove the bones and serve, without straining, in a warm soup tureen. Serve crisp croutons to sprinkle on the top.

SERVES 4–6

You may add slices of frankfurter or crisp bacon bits or slivers of ham shortly before the soup is done.

If you like this as well as we do, you will make a meal of it. But, of course, you may serve it in soup cups as a first course.

SPLIT PEA SOUP

2   cups dried split peas
6   cups cold water
1   ham bone
¼   lb salt pork, cut in pieces
10 cups water
2   medium onions, diced
1   cup chopped celery leaves and stalks

Soak the peas overnight in the 6 cups of cold water. Drain and put in a heavy soup kettle with the ham bone, salt pork, and 10 cups of water. Cover and simmer 2 hours, then add the onions and celery. Simmer about 1 hour longer, adding another cup of water if needed. Put the soup through a strainer, or use the blender. If it is not thick enough, add ½ cup of light cream.

SERVES 4–6

A little dry sherry or rosé wine may be added if you like. And a garnish of paper-thin lemon slices is a good idea. This makes a fine supper with a crisp salad, crusty Italian bread, and melon or any fruit in season.

BARBARA'S MINESTRONE

1 lb summer squash, sliced thin	1 cup thin spaghetti, broken in 2" lengths
1 lb zucchini, sliced thin	
2 cups fresh green cabbage, cut in 1" strips or squares	1 No. 2 can tomatoes and juice, or 2 cups fresh tomatoes
3 large onions, diced	3 tbsp olive oil
¼ lb salt pork	Salt and pepper to taste
1 pkg frozen cut green beans	¼ tsp garlic salt, or to taste
1 cup fresh or frozen green peas (never canned)	

The whole point in making this soup is to keep the vegetables from becoming mushy and to retain their color and texture.

Prepare the first 4 vegetables and have at hand. Mince salt pork finely and put in heavy stewpot over low heat. As fat accumulates, add diced onions and cook until soft and yellow, not brown. Add 1 to 2 quarts of water; add squash, zucchini, and green beans. Simmer. Meanwhile, cook peas separately in very little water. Drain and have at hand. Cook spaghetti separately until almost done. Drain and have at hand.

When squash and beans are almost done, add tomatoes and juice, bring back to boil, add cabbage, and cook 8 to 10 minutes more. Add peas and spaghetti. Add olive oil, salt and pepper, and garlic salt.

Sprinkle with Parmesan cheese, and serve with hot crusty bread.

SERVES 6–8

This is Barbara Lovely's recipe and is the best minestrone I ever ate. I have enjoyed minestrone in many Italian restaurants that were famous for it, but this version surpasses them all, in my opinion. The Lovelys' house on Cape Cod is within sound of the sea, and if a window is open, the smell of salt and of piny woods drifts in. Conversation in the beautiful dining room is temporarily hushed, for the first taste of this soup takes precedence over the most lively opinions.

POTATO SOUP SPECIAL

¼ lb bacon
¼ lb leeks, finely diced
1   medium or 2 small onions, diced
    Butter
2   qts chicken bouillon or stock
½ lb white potatoes, diced
1   pint milk
1   pint light cream
    Seasoned salt and pepper to taste
    Chopped fresh parsley

Sauté the bacon, leeks, and onion, adding some butter to the drippings. Add to the chicken stock, then add potatoes. Cook about 25 minutes. Add milk, cream, salt, and pepper, and let the soup heat but not boil. Sprinkle parsley on top and serve in warm bowls.

SERVES 10

On an icy winter day, this soup is always welcome. Serve with crisp cucumber salad and a bowl of croutons and strong hot coffee. Incidentally, there is nothing worse than hot soup that is lukewarm or cold soup that isn't frosty cold. Too often, in otherwise good restaurants, the soup is not hot enough or cold enough, as the case may be. This potato soup may be served cold in August. Chill the bowls in the refrigerator. I make my own croutons by dicing almost-stale bread, and placing it on a cookie tray in a warm oven. I turn it with a spatula until the cubes are golden brown. I use these croutons in tossed salads too.

BASIC LEEK AND POTATO SOUP

Fresh leeks (white part only) and
    white onions, diced to make 3 cups
3 tbsp butter
3 tbsp flour
    Hot water, about 4 cups
4 cups diced or cubed potatoes
1 tsp seasoned salt
    The green part of the leeks, chopped
    Milk to make the consistency you like

Cook leeks and onions in butter for 5 minutes, until golden but not brown. Add flour and cook 2 minutes, stirring until blended. Remove from heat and add the hot water, then the potatoes, salt, and the green part of the leeks (you may not want to use all the green). Simmer for 30 to 40 minutes, then add milk slowly to thicken the soup. Do not let it boil.

SERVES 4–6

This is a basic leek soup. Serve in hot soup bowls and sprinkle with chopped parsley or chives. It is the most versatile soup, for you may add 3 cubes of squash with the potatoes, or a few green beans, or Brussels sprouts, or a few lettuce leaves. You may put it through a sieve for a creamy soup or leave it as is if you like the potato chunks.

PUMPKIN SOUP

2   lbs pumpkin, peeled and diced
½   lb fresh tomatoes, peeled and diced
1   potato, peeled and diced
1   onion, peeled and diced
4   cups water
½   cup cream
1   tbsp butter

Place the vegetables and water in a heavy kettle and cook about 20 minutes or until tender. Drain and purée the mixture in your blender or put through a sieve. Heat again, add cream and butter, and bring just to a boil. Serve with croutons.

SERVES 4–6

If you happen to like pumpkin and an unusual soup, this is a treat. I love it.

RUSSIAN ICY SHRIMP SOUP

½ lb shrimp, cooked and shelled
2   medium cucumbers (about 1½ cups),
        peeled, seeded, and diced
2   cups sour cream
5   cups buttermilk
½ cup sauerkraut juice
2   cloves garlic, chopped
    Salt and white pepper to taste
3   tbsp finely chopped fresh dill (or 2 tbsp dried)
½ cup fresh finely chopped fennel (or 1 tsp dried)
½ cup finely chopped scallions
2   hard-cooked eggs, finely chopped

Parboil the shrimps for 3 to 5 minutes, then let them cool in their own liquid. Marinate the cucumbers in 1 teaspoon of salt for at least half an hour to extract the excess moisture. Now in a stainless steel or glass bowl, combine sour cream, buttermilk, sauerkraut juice, garlic, salt, and pepper. Beat with a wire whisk until smooth. Add the remaining ingredients except the eggs. Fold in and refrigerate overnight. Chill soup plates or cups in the freezer about an hour before you are ready to serve. Then serve the soup with a teaspoon of the chopped egg on each serving.

SERVES 4–6—or more, depending on the size of the soup plates

Kay Mack makes this delectable soup often and says she loves it, especially because it can be made ahead—indeed, it must be!

TOMATO BOUILLON

2 cups tomato juice
1 bouillon cube
2 slices onion
1 bay leaf, crumbled
1 whole clove
¼ tsp celery salt
Salt and pepper to taste
Lemon slices

Mix tomato juice with bouillon cube, onion, bay leaf, clove, and seasonings. Simmer 15 minutes. Add a dash of Tabasco if you wish. Strain into hot soup cups. Top with lemon slices (or sour cream if you prefer).

SERVES 2

I like to make a large quantity of this and store it in the refrigerator. It lends added charm to almost any company supper and is fine for luncheon with sandwiches or crab salad.

JAMIE MAYER'S CHUNKY TURKY SOUP IMPROVEMENTS

This recipe is exactly as Jamie sent it to me and I wouldn't want a letter changed.

> 1 large can chunky turky soup
> 1 carrot sliced up
> 1 shake Worchestire sause
> 3 or 4 shakes of onion, plain, and garlic salt
> 1 crushed boullion cube
>   Lots of pepper (9 or 10 grinds)

Then boil to taste.

SERVES 2–4

As I write, Jamie has acquired his first complete football accouterment at age fifteen. In the past he and I have watched a good many football games on television, explaining the plays to each other. His father, the son of Jill, my housemate at Stillmeadow for many years, grew up at Stillmeadow. I am glad to see his son take an interest in cooking!

SOUP OF THE EVENING, BEAUTIFUL SOUP

2   lbs beef brisket
1   beef soup bone
2   qts liquid (water, or beef bouillon and
        water, or water with a couple of
        bouillon cubes dissolved in it)
3   tsp seasoned salt
    Pepper to taste
1   cup chopped onion
1   cup chopped green pepper
2   carrots, cut in 1½" cubes
1   cup sliced celery
1   cup peeled, diced potatoes
1   large can tomatoes
½   lb zucchini, diced

Place the meat, bone, liquid, salt, and pepper in a large, heavy soup
kettle or Dutch oven. Cover and bring to a boil, skim the foam off,
simmer for 2 hours, or until the meat is tender. Remove soup from
the heat and chill thoroughly to let the fat harden (overnight is fine).
Then discard the fat and add the vegetables (except the zucchini)
and simmer about 1 hour. Remove from heat and take out the bone
(I hope you have a nice dog, as this is a safe bone). Take out the
meat and cut in small cubes. Add meat and zucchini to the soup and
bring to a boil, then simmer 5 or 10 minutes.

SERVES 6–8

*As with most soups, you can use your imagination. I like to add a
dollop of tomato paste or a few leftover mixed vegetables such as
peas and beans. And a spoonful of Worcestershire sauce or Kitchen
Bouquet adds zest.*

*Serve with crusty French garlic bread and a mixed green salad with
Italian dressing for a party dinner. Be sure the soup tureen is hot, the
soup bowls warm.*

VICHYSSOISE

2 cups diced raw potatoes
2 cups diced leeks or onions
1 cup chicken broth
1 cup sour cream
1 tsp Worcestershire sauce
   Seasoned salt to taste
1 tbsp chopped chives

Cook potatoes and leeks in very little water until soft. Press through a food mill or beat in a blender until soft, then add the broth and let cool. Add sour cream and beat well. Add seasoning and chill. Serve in individual cups topped with chives.

SERVES 4–5

This is a delicate and delightful cold soup. You can keep it in the refrigerator for several days, adding the sour cream before serving.

VICHYSSOISE PARISIENNE

4 leeks
1 medium-sized onion, thinly sliced
1 medium-sized carrot, thinly sliced
2 stalks celery, chopped fine
½ cup butter
5 cups chicken broth or consommé
1 cup dry white wine
2 tbsp chopped parsley
5 medium-sized potatoes, peeled and thinly sliced
3 cups light cream
  Seasoned salt and pepper to taste
  Dash of cayenne pepper
  Pinch of mace
1 cup heavy cream
  Minced chives

Slice the white part of the leeks and sauté with the onion, carrot, and celery in butter until lightly brown, 10 minutes or so. In a heavy pot or kettle place the chicken broth or consommé, wine, parsley, and potatoes. Add the sautéed vegetables and simmer about 30 minutes. Strain into a saucepan. Force through a sieve or use your blender, then add the light cream and seasonings and bring to a boil, but do not overcook. Remove from fire and chill in the refrigerator. Just before serving, add the heavy cream, well chilled, and beat with a wire whisk or rotary beater for 1 or 2 minutes. Serve in chilled bowls topped with minced chives.

SERVES 4–6

This may well be the queen of soups.

TRADITIONAL VICHYSSOISE

3 medium-sized leeks
1 medium-sized onion
2 tbsp butter or margarine
4 medium-sized potatoes, sliced very thin
4 cups chicken broth or clear chicken stock
1–2 cups cream
   Seasoned salt and white pepper
   Chopped chives

Sauté leeks and onion in the butter, then add potatoes and chicken broth. Simmer, covered, for about 15 minutes, or until tender. Put through a sieve or blend in your electric blender until smooth. Add cream and seasonings. Chill thoroughly and serve, sprinkled with chives, in cups.

SERVES 6

This is the super soup for hot August weather. You may make it ahead in what is supposed to be the cool of the day.

EGGS AND CHEESE

EGGS BENEDICT

1 hard-cooked egg	Seasoned salt and cayenne
4 slices cooked ham	pepper to taste
½ cup and 1 tbsp butter	4 toast rounds
3 egg yolks	4 poached eggs
3 tbsp lemon juice	Parsley

Put the hard-cooked egg yolk through a sieve and chop the white. Trim the sliced ham to make four 3″ rounds. Mince or grind the trimmings. Heat the chopped white, yolk, and ham trimmings in a double boiler. Melt 1 tablespoon of butter in a pan and warm the ham rounds

63

in it. Meanwhile heat the ½ cup of butter. Beat the raw egg yolks, lemon juice, and seasonings (on low speed if you use a blender). Slowly add the butter and blend until smooth, then stir in the hard-cooked egg and ham mixture.

Put 2 toast rounds on each of 2 plates and top them with a slice of ham and a poached egg. Spoon the sauce over and garnish with parsley.

SERVES 2

This is supposed to have been invented by Commodore Benedict, and that is all I know about him. It is one of those elegant dishes for a special twosome when you and the man in your life have a quiet supper by an open fire. Sliced ripe tomatoes sprinkled with frozen dried chives belong with it.

STILLMEADOW BAKED EGGS

    1 can cream-style corn (large size)
      Seasoned salt and pepper to taste
    4 green pepper rings
    4 eggs
    1 tbsp bread crumbs
    2 tbsp grated Parmesan cheese
      Paprika
      Butter

Season the corn and place in individual greased ramekins. Parboil pepper rings for 5 minutes, then place a ring in each ramekin. Now break the eggs carefully into the rings, sprinkle with bread crumbs, cheese, and paprika. Dot with butter. Bake 15 minutes in a moderate (350°) oven, or until the eggs are set.

SERVES 4

A delightful Sunday morning breakfast with corn muffins or buttered toast.

SUNDAY SCRAMBLED EGGS

2 tbsp butter
1 3-oz pkg cream cheese
  Cream
  Seasoned salt, pepper, and paprika
  Grated Swiss cheese to taste
2 truffles, minced (if you can get them)
4 eggs

Melt the butter in a heavy frying pan and stir in the cream cheese until smooth. Add cream enough to make the sauce as thin as you like. Add seasonings. Add Swiss cheese and truffles (I use mushrooms when I have no truffles). Break the eggs in the sauce and stir with a silver fork. When they are creamy, serve on hot buttered toast points.

SERVES 4, but double it for 6

SPANISH SCRAMBLED EGGS

4 tbsp butter
½ cup sliced mushrooms
2 oz dry sherry
1 medium-sized onion, diced
½ tsp chili powder
6 eggs
½ tsp seasoned salt
3 tbsp cream

Heat half of the butter in a saucepan, add the mushrooms, and sauté until tender—about 10 minutes. Blend in the sherry and keep warm. Meanwhile put the rest of the butter in a skillet, add onion and chili powder. When the onions are transparent and golden, add mushroom and sherry mixture, then the eggs, slightly beaten. Add seasonings and cream, and stir until fluffy and just set (don't overcook). Serve on toast triangles.

SERVES 4-6

TRADITIONAL OMELET

4	eggs
¼	cup light cream
1½	tbsp butter
½	tsp seasoned salt
	Paprika to taste

Have the eggs at room temperature before you begin. Beat them with a fork, not a beater. Blend in the cream (or top milk if you wish). Melt the butter in a skillet or omelet pan, and when it is hot but not brown, add the eggs. Cook over low heat, lifting the edges with a pancake turner or spatula and tilting the pan to let the uncooked part run to the bottom. When the omelet is just set, fold it over and season. Serve at once.

SERVES 4

Omelets are probably the most controversial of all dishes. Some experts feel only individual omelets are worth making. So you would make 4 for 4 diners. As for the seasoning, salt does toughen eggs, so it is probably a good idea to add it at the last minute. As with most egg dishes, overcooking is the most common mistake. The omelet will go on cooking itself after you fold it over. Controversial, but oh, so versatile. Any filling you like may be folded in—from spinach to lobster (see next recipe). Also plain old chili sauce is popular at my house, just a dollop tossed in. Chopped chives or mushrooms do no harm. Or try shredded dried beef or wafers of ham—suit your own taste.

LOBSTER OMELET STILLMEADOW

5 eggs	1 tbsp milk
1 tbsp butter	Pinch of paprika
1 tbsp flour	Seasoned salt and pepper
1 cup chicken broth	1 tsp chopped parsley
1 cup light cream	1 can lobster meat—or cooked
2 tbsp dry sherry	fresh if you have it
1 egg yolk	

Melt butter in a heavy saucepan and blend the flour in, then add chicken broth, cream, and sherry. When the mixture is smooth and thickened, remove from heat and stir in the egg yolk mixed with the tablespoon of milk. Add seasonings and parsley. Sauté the lobster meat, cut in pieces, in butter until heated, then add to the sauce. Keep warm over very low heat but do not let it come to a boil. Keep warm while you make the omelet, allowing 1 egg per person plus 1 extra for the pan. Lift the omelet gently to a warm platter and pour the lobster sauce over.

SERVES 4

This is for special birthday breakfasts or brunches. Serve with toast points.

DAISY EGGS

1 egg to a person
    Seasoned salt, paprika, and Worcestershire
        sauce to taste

Separate the yolks from the whites and keep each yolk in an individual dish. Beat the whites well and add the seasonings. Spoon the whites carefully into flat greased ramekins or pile them in individual mounds on a greased baking sheet. Slip the yolks in each white and bake in a moderate oven (325°) until the yolks are set and the whites begin to brown.

This recipe is elegant with corn muffins or popovers and is fine for brunch or a holiday breakfast. In my childhood, it was my get-well treat. We used to have what was called grippe in midwinter, and Mama stopped taking my temperature when I sat up and asked if I couldn't have Daisy Eggs for my supper.

EGGS IN ASPIC

2   envelopes unflavored gelatin
½   cup cold water
4   cups chicken broth or consommé
1   tbsp dried tarragon
8   eggs
½   cup liver pâté or deviled ham
    Mayonnaise
    Dry mustard

Soak gelatin in the cold water for 5 minutes. Heat the consommé and dissolve the gelatin in it. Cool. Cover the bottom of a mold (or use 8 custard cups or individual ramekins) with a layer of gelatin. Sprinkle the tarragon over. Poach the eggs, trim the edges, and let them cool. When the gelatin is slightly firm, slip the eggs in carefully. Spread them lightly with the pâté or ham. Spoon remaining gelatin over and chill in the refrigerator until firm. Turn out on a bed of shredded greens. Season the mayonnaise with the mustard (you may like a lot as I do). Serve in a bowl with aspic. Garnish with watercress.

SERVES 8

This is another recipe I have shared with unnumbered friends and is one of the best summer luncheon entrées I know.

CARACAS EGGS

4   oz shredded dried beef
2   tbsp butter
1   tsp chili powder
½   lb grated American cheese
2   cups stewed tomatoes
6   beaten eggs
    Seasoned salt and pepper to taste

Place the dried beef in a heavy skillet with the butter, chili powder, cheese, and tomatoes. Cook over low heat, stirring until the mixture bubbles. Add the eggs, and continue stirring until it thickens. Serve on thin slices of buttered toast.

SERVES 4–6

Serve with a tossed salad and extra toast and hot coffee for a gala brunch.

CREOLE EGGS

6 eggs, slightly beaten
4 or 5 mushrooms, sliced
1 tbsp diced onion
  Butter
1 cup peeled, chopped tomatoes
1 tsp capers, if desired

Sauté the mushrooms and onion in butter until golden. Add the tomatoes and cook about 8 minutes. Pour the mixture in the blazer of the chafing dish, add remaining ingredients. Put the blazer over hot water in the lower container and stir gently (use a wooden spoon if possible). When the eggs are creamy, serve at once over buttered toast triangles.

SERVES 4

There are many variations for Creole Eggs, such as adding diced sweet pepper or a few pitted black olives. If good fresh tomatoes are not in season, use canned, draining off some of the juice. You don't want egg soup.

EGGS ESPAGNOLE

4   hard-cooked eggs, sliced lengthwise and with yolks removed
½   cup mayonnaise
½   cup grated Cheddar cheese
½   tsp dry mustard
1   tsp vinegar
2   packages frozen asparagus tips
1   can mushroom soup
1   cup milk
⅓   cup bread crumbs mixed with 2 tbsp melted butter

Mix yolks well with the mayonnaise, cheese, mustard, and vinegar. Stuff the whites with the yolk mixture. Place the asparagus tips in a greased casserole. Arrange eggs in a star pattern on the asparagus tips. Mix mushroom soup and milk and simmer about 5 minutes. Pour this over the casserole. Top with bread crumbs. Bake 20 minutes in a moderate oven (350°).

SERVES 4

You may make this ahead of time. It is good with a salad of raw vegetables and French dressing.

EGGS MORNAY

2   tbsp butter
2   tbsp flour
    Seasoned salt and pepper to taste
½   tsp Worcestershire sauce
1   tsp prepared mustard (I like Dijon mustard for this)
2   cups milk
⅓   cup grated Cheddar cheese
6   eggs
    Paprika

Melt the butter, blend in the flour and seasonings, and gradually add milk, stirring constantly. When the sauce is smooth, add the cheese and stir until melted. Put a layer of the cheese sauce in a flat glass baking dish or casserole. Slide the eggs in gently, cover partially with remaining sauce, dust with paprika, and bake in a moderate oven (350°) for about 20 minutes, or until the yolks are firm, the sauce bubbly.

SERVES 4–6

Individual ramekins are nice to use for this too. Serve this dish for brunch with buttered toast triangles and a romaine salad and coffee.

CHEESE SOUFFLÉ

4   tbsp butter
4   tbsp flour
1   cup milk
½   tsp seasoned salt
    Dash of cayenne pepper
1   cup grated sharp cheese
4   egg yolks, beaten until light
5   egg whites, beaten until stiff

Melt the butter, blend in the flour, and add the milk gradually. Stir until thick and smooth, then add seasonings and cheese. Remove from heat and gently add egg yolks and let cool. Then stir a little of the egg whites into the mixture and fold in the rest gently. Spoon into an ungreased 1½ -quart soufflé baking dish (or a straight-sided casserole). Set in a pan of hot water and bake 25 to 30 minutes at 325°, or until puffed and golden.

SERVES 4

Plan to have this when you are not looking down the road to see when the guests will arrive. The best of soufflés will sag if kept waiting.

CHEESE SOUFFLÉ À LA FRANÇAISE

4½   tbsp flour
3½   tbsp butter
1½   cups heated milk
6   egg yolks
      Salt, pepper, and cayenne pepper
2   or 3 drops hot sauce to taste
8   egg whites
¼   tsp cream of tartar
1   cup grated Swiss cheese

Blend the flour and butter and cook over moderate heat about 2 minutes or until mixture begins to froth; add milk gradually and beat with a wire whisk for 1 minute, or until it bubbles. Beat in the egg yolks gradually, add seasonings. Now beat 6 egg whites until stiff, add 2 more, and beat, adding the cream of tartar while beating, and an extra pinch of salt. Fold carefully into the first mixture, adding the cheese at the same time. Bake in a 375° oven for 40 to 45 minutes in an 8-cup buttered mold or deep, straight-sided casserole. Put a collar of foil around the top of the mold to keep the soufflé in bounds. Do not peek in for at least 20 minutes or you will regret it!

SERVES 4–6

As with most egg and cheese dishes, have everything at room temperature before you begin.

SWISS CHEESE FONDUE

1 clove garlic, split
1 lb Swiss cheese, finely cut
3 tbsp flour
2 cups dry white wine (Rhine or Chablis or Riesling)
   Salt and pepper to taste
6 tbsp Kirschwasser or cognac

Rub the garlic around the earthenware fondue dish. Dredge cheese in flour. (European experts use potato flour, but I never seem to have any!) Pour wine in the dish and heat almost to boiling, then add cheese and seasonings. Stir constantly with a wooden spoon until the fondue begins to bubble, then add the Kirsch or cognac. Keep the fondue hot over the fondue lamp.

SERVES 6–8

Serve with a bowl of French or Italian bread cut in cubes so each cube has one side of crust. You need long-handled fondue forks so that each diner can dip the bread in the fondue. Meanwhile keep the fondue hot. Fondue sets are available in most stores now, even in some drugstores, but you can manage with an old-fashioned chafing dish if you have to. Use real cheese, not processed, for this. Fondue is a meal in itself and one of the best.

MILLIE'S CHEESE AND ONION TART

Pastry to line a 9″ pie tin (you may use a mix or
    make your own)
4   cups thinly sliced Spanish onions
3   tbsp butter
3   eggs
1½ cups light cream (or undiluted evaporated milk)
¼   tsp Worcestershire sauce
4   slices bacon
1   cup shredded Swiss or Cheddar cheese

Line the pie tin with the pastry and flute the edges well. A deep pie
tin is best. Place in refrigerator. Cut the sliced onions in half. Melt
butter in a frying pan and slowly cook the onions in it until they are
transparent. Cool. Beat eggs slightly and add cream and Worcestershire sauce. Cook the bacon in another pan until crisp. Drain. Now
place cooled onions in the pie tin and sprinkle cheese over. Pour the
custard over all. Bake at 400° for about 40 minutes, or until a knife
inserted in the center comes out clean. Garnish with bacon.

SERVES 4–6

*Whenever I am going to Millie and Ed's for supper and she says she
can't think what to have, Ed and I speak in unison: "Have onion pie."*

QUICHE LORRAINE

1½   cups sifted flour
½   tsp salt
¼   lb butter or margarine
     Ice water
4   eggs
2   cups thin cream
1   cup grated Swiss cheese
     Dash each of sugar, cayenne pepper, seasoned salt, seasoned
        pepper (¾ tsp salt if the cheese is very mild)
12   strips bacon, broiled until crisp and drained on a paper towel

Sift flour and salt and work the butter in until the mixture looks like cornmeal. Sprinkle on enough ice water to make the dough hold its shape (around 4 tablespoons). Shape into a ball and chill in refrigerator about an hour, then roll out on a lightly floured board, fitting it into a 10″ pie plate (preferably Pyrex). Trim and crimp edges, prick with fork, and place in refrigerator.

Preheat oven to 450°. Break eggs into a bowl and add cream, cheese, and seasonings. Rub a little soft butter over the pastry and sprinkle bacon over, then pour the egg mixture over all. Bake at 450° for 12 minutes, reduce heat to 325°, and bake until a knife inserted in the center comes out clean.

SERVES 4—or 8 for cocktail wedges

I first had this in Newton, Connecticut, at a dear friend's house. We had a crisp salad and white wine with it, and I took the recipe right home with me. Much as I hate rolling pastry, it is worth it!

EASY WELSH RABBIT

1 bottle beer or ale
1 tbsp butter
1 lb sharp cheese, diced
1 tbsp dry mustard
1 tbsp Worcestershire sauce
   Dash of cayenne pepper
   Paprika

Open the beer beforehand and let it stand. When ready to serve, melt the butter in the blazer of a chafing dish or in a heavy pan. Add cheese and very gently melt it, but never overcook it. Add the seasonings as the cheese melts, and then slowly add the beer, stirring in one direction only. When the mixture is smooth and blended, serve at once over dry toast wedges. Dusted with paprika.

SERVES 4-6

This is an elegant supper on a winter night and very easy to do. As with all cheese dishes, you simply must be careful not to let the cheese boil up and get stringy.

SCOTCH WOODCOCK

6 slices thin toast
Anchovy paste
6 eggs, beaten
3 tbsp butter
3 tbsp light cream
2 tbsp catsup
3 tbsp chopped parsley
Seasoned salt and pepper to taste

Spread the toast with the anchovy paste. Scramble the eggs with butter and cream, add catsup, parsley, and seasonings. Spread 2 tablespoons of the egg mixture on the toast slices and serve hot at once.

SERVES 4–6

But 3 will eat it if they have a chance! This is a fine New Year's morning dish. Its origin goes way back, but whether it is really Scotch, who knows?

FROM THE SEA

BAKED STUFFED FISH

1	3–5-lb fish—haddock, blue-fish, bass, or cod, cleaned, scaled, and eviscerated	2	tbsp chopped onion
		½	cup chopped celery
		2	tbsp chopped parsley
	Butter	1	egg, beaten
	French dressing (optional)		Seasoned salt and pepper
	Sauterne		Paprika
	Stuffing:		Milk or melted butter
1½	cups bread crumbs		

Mix the stuffing ingredients well and stuff the fish lightly. Place fish in a shallow baking pan on foil. Cut a couple of gashes along each side to keep it from curling up. Bake about 40 minutes in a hot oven (400°), or until it flakes when tested with a fork. Baste with melted butter or French dressing (not the thick commercial kind). Add equal parts of butter and sauterne and heat for a sauce.

Garnish with lemon wedges, ripe olives, parsley, or whatever you feel like using.

SERVES 4–6

BROILED SWORDFISH STEAKS

½ lb fish per serving

Preheat the broiler and brush rack with butter. Brush steaks well with melted butter. Put the rack about 6 inches from the broiling unit and broil the steaks 5 minutes. Baste with melted butter, turn, and broil 5 to 8 minutes more. Serve with horseradish if you like it.

Swordfish can be either delicious or very dry and flat. The secret is in using a lot of butter. Sprinkle the steaks with freshly grated or seasoned pepper and salt and dried parsley before serving. Serve with broiled tomatoes sprinkled with freeze-dried or freshly chopped chives and a green salad.

Swordfish steaks are extra good done on the outdoor grill over charcoal. And better yet, the kitchen does not smell of broiling fish!

CAPE COD BAKED FLOUNDER

2 small flounder fillets per person, or 1 large one
  Corn-flake crumbs
  Seasoned salt and pepper
  Melted butter to cover
½ cup milk per person

Sprinkle the crumbs over the fish. Lay the fillets in a foil-lined baking pan. Dust with salt and pepper and pour the melted butter and milk over. Bake at 350° for about 20 minutes, or until the fish flakes easily. If you wish, you may turn the broiler on briefly to brown the fish.

Garnish with lemon wedges. Serve with rice and a green salad.

STEAMED SOFT-SHELLED CLAMS

2 dozen unshucked clams per person
½" water—or less
  Melted butter
  Lemon wedges, if you must

Scrub clams thoroughly with a brush and rinse in fresh water. Put them in a large kettle or in a steamer. Add the water. Cover tightly and steam over moderate heat just until the shells open—5 or 10 minutes. Put the clams in warm bowls. Strain the broth into cups and serve to each guest a cup of broth and a cup of melted butter.

Some people dip the clams in the broth first, then in the butter; others reverse the process. I alternate. I let the lemon alone.

My neighbor Pret often brings me a bucket of clams from our beach. He washes them in seawater before he leaves the shore. When you have fresh sweet clams, you do not need anything else except coffee. You just eat clams and sip the broth. My friend Slim can eat 4 dozen.

BAKED STUFFED CLAMS

17½-oz can minced clams,
  drained
2   tbsp melted butter
¼   cup seasoned bread crumbs
⅓   cup clam juice
½   tsp lemon juice
½   tsp salt

¼   tsp each: basil, marjoram,
  thyme
Few drops Worcestershire
  sauce
Butter
Grated Parmesan cheese
Paprika

Mix well all but the last 3 ingredients. Spread in clam shells, dot with butter, cheese, and paprika. Freeze. To serve, heat in 350° oven for 20 minutes. Let cool slightly before serving.

SERVES 4–6

SAM'S CLAMS

5–6 quahogs per person
1   slice sharp Cheddar cheese per quahog
1–2 small pieces bacon per quahog

Preheat the oven to 450°. Open the quahogs, cherrystone size or larger, scooping all the meat into one half of each shell (as if for eating on the half-shell). Set the quahogs on foil in a large baking pan. Place a slice of cheese, then bacon pieces on each quahog. Bake for 10 minutes for the small size (2″ to 3″ across) and 15 minutes or more for the larger quahogs.

This comes from the Johnsons, and Polly calls it the most wonderful lunch. But it makes a fine supper dish too, with crusty garlic bread and a salad.

MINCED CLAM FRITTERS À LA PACIFIC NORTHWEST

3 eggs, well beaten
  Seasoned salt and pepper
2 tsp instant onion flakes
1 can minced clams (or you may use fresh)
16 soda crackers, crushed fine
  Salad oil

Add salt, pepper, and onion flakes to eggs, then add clams. Blend in the crackers and stir. Drop by spoonfuls into hot salad oil. Turn once.

SERVES 4

Frances, who sent me this, always serves a fruit salad with the fritters, and a light dessert if any. For lunch or supper, it is always a hit.

Frances and I never meet, being so far apart, but we exchange recipes and keep the mails busy!

ELAINE'S CLAMS LINGUINI

Garlic butter
Clams
Celery salt and paprika
Linguini

Sauté the clams in garlic butter until the edges curl, then add celery salt and paprika. Keep the clams warm. Boil the linguini exactly 12 minutes in salted water to cover.

Serve the linguini in soup bowls. Add as much clam broth as you wish to the clams and bring just to a boil. Pour over the pasta and top with chopped parsley.

For this recipe, you have to judge your own quantity, but there won't be any left over in any case.

SYLVIA GIBSON'S CLAM PIE

2 cups chopped clams
½ cup clam liquor
½ cup milk
1 egg, well beaten
½ cup cracker crumbs
  Pastry for double-crust 9″ pie

Mix the first 5 ingredients and put into pastry-lined pie tin. Dot with 2 tablespoons of butter. Add the top crust and prick a few holes in it. Bake in a 375° oven for about an hour and a quarter.

SERVES 4–6

Sylvia and Jim live around the corner from me on Cape Cod. Jim is a dedicated fisherman and brings home many gifts from the sea. And there are always clams on our beach at Mill Pond!

IONE'S QUICK-AND-EASY CLAM PIE

1 can (15 oz) Howard Johnson's New England Clam Chowder, as it
    comes from the can
1 can (7½ oz) Snow's Minced Clams, lightly drained
  Pinch or so of thyme
  Dried onion flakes to taste
  Parsley, fresh or flakes
  Pastry for double-crust 9″ pie

Mix the first 5 ingredients and put into pastry-lined pie tin. (Betty Crocker's piecrust mix is easy and good.) Dot with butter, put on top crust, and seal edges. Slash top crust here and there.

SERVES 4

The nice thing about this is that it can come from your emergency shelf. Add a tossed salad and coffee, and you are set for a happy supper.

SPAGHETTI WITH CLAM SAUCE

2 dozen cherrystone clams in the shell
¼ cup olive oil
3 tbsp butter
3 cloves garlic, minced
2 leeks, chopped
¼ cup chopped parsley
    Dash of rosemary
½ cup dry white wine
    Seasoned pepper and salt to taste
1 pound spaghetti, cooked al dente

Open the clams as best you can, reserve them and 1 cup of clam juice. Chop clams—you should have almost a cup. Heat oil and butter and add garlic and leeks. Cook until golden, then add parsley, rosemary, clam juice, and white wine. Bring to a boil, add pepper and a dash of salt (remember, the clams are salty). Simmer about 15 minutes, add chopped clams, and cook 5 minutes more. Serve over spaghetti.

SERVES 4

If you cannot get clams in the shell, use canned clams. Serve a dry white wine with this and that inevitable tossed salad. You need nothing fancier than fresh fruit for dessert, with coffee.

SALT CODFISH CAKES

    Frozen codfish fillets
    Vinegar or lemon juice
4   large potatoes (or 1 potato for each serving)
4   tbsp butter
    Chopped onion (optional)
    Pepper
    Herbs to taste
1   egg
    Flour
    Yellow cornmeal (optional)
    Fat for frying

Soak codfish fillets in cold water to which a little vinegar or lemon juice has been added. Change the water once or twice while fillets are thawing, then cook in fresh water with same amount of vinegar or lemon juice to cover, about 20 minutes. Boil the potatoes in their jackets, then peel and mash with butter, pepper, and herbs. Drain the cooked fish and add to potatoes, mashing all together. Now add the egg and whip well. Flour your hands and make cakes, whatever size you prefer (we like them small). Pat on some yellow cornmeal if you want them to be pretty! Fry in hot fat until golden brown.

SERVES 4

Serve plain on hot plates. Caesar salad goes well with this. You may add a little chopped onion to the fish. This makes a wonderful Sunday breakfast or a winter supper any day.

SALT CODFISH PARMENTIER

1   lb salt cod
1½   cups Béchamel Sauce
3   cups mashed potatoes
2   tbsp finely diced cheese (natural Swiss is best)
2   tsp butter

Cover the fish with cold water and soak 12 hours, or overnight. Change the water several times. Cover fish with fresh water and simmer gently until it flakes, but do not boil. Prepare Béchamel Sauce (see "Sauces and Salad Dressings"). Add the fish. Butter a 6-cup baking dish and spread half the potatoes in it. Add the fish with the sauce. Cover with remaining potatoes and sprinkle with cheese. Dot with butter. Bake in a 400° oven about 15 minutes, or until brown and bubbly.

SERVES 6

Have the mashed potatoes light and fluffy. Instant mashed are good for this when potatoes are not at their best. This is such a delightful dish and kind to the budget, if you are smart enough to have one.

In my childhood, most people in Appleton, Wisconsin, bought salt codfish in those little wooden boxes that were shipped from the East. The pantry shelves always had a good supply.

MARYLAND CRAB PANCAKE

For each serving you use the following:	3 tbsp lukewarm water
3 eggs	½ tbsp chopped parsley
4 drops Tabasco	½ tbsp chopped chives
¼ tsp seasoned salt	3 heaping tbsp cooked crab meat
¼ tsp seasoned pepper	1 tbsp butter

Break the eggs into a small bowl, add Tabasco, salt, pepper, and water. Beat lightly, using a fork. Add parsley, chives, and crab meat. Get a heavy skillet sizzling hot, then melt butter in it. Pour in egg mixture and cook like an omelet for about 1 minute, until it is set but not brown. Slide onto a warm plate.

If you are not able to have freshly cooked crab, use canned or frozen cooked crab meat. An old-fashioned cast-iron skillet is perfect for these pancakes, but the electric frying pan is fine too. This makes an elegant brunch when friends drop in on a weekend.

CHEESE AND CRAB FONDUE

1 large can of crab meat or lobster, or 1 small can of each
1 cup chopped celery
3 tbsp mayonnaise mixed with 1 tbsp prepared mustard and dash of chives
Salt and paprika to taste
4 or 6 slices bread
Sliced Swiss or American cheese
2 well-beaten eggs mixed with 1 cup milk and a dash of Worcestershire sauce

Mix first 4 ingredients and spread between slices of bread, then cut in two. Layer in a greased casserole, with slices of cheese between the layers. Pour over the egg mixture. Cover and bake for 40 minutes in a moderate oven (325°). Serve with green salad and hot buttery corn bread.

SERVES 4–6

For unexpected company, this is an easy answer, provided you aren't just out of bread! It is also very flexible; you can serve more if you add another can of lobster or crab meat, another egg, and a little more milk. If you happen to have leftover fresh shellfish, you can use that, but who ever has leftover lobster or crab meat? Well, now and then!

CREAMED CRAB AND MUSHROOMS

1   8-oz can sliced mushrooms
⅓ cup butter
1   tbsp chopped chives
2   tbsp chopped onion (I use the frozen for this)
1   tbsp chopped parsley
⅓ cup flour
    Salt and cayenne pepper to taste
1   cup mushroom liquid (add milk
        if needed to make up the cupful)
3   egg yolks, slightly beaten
1   large can flaked crab meat
2   cups sour cream
2   tbsp dry sherry

Sauté mushrooms in butter with chives, onion, and parsley. Blend in seasonings and flour, and stir over low heat until smooth and bubbly. Remove from heat and stir in the liquid, boil for 1 minute. Remove from heat again and stir slowly into beaten egg yolks. Last, stir in crab meat, sour cream, and sherry. Bring just to boiling and serve at once in toasted bread cups.

TOASTED BREAD CUPS

Brush thinly sliced bread (with crusts removed) with melted butter. Press into muffin cups. Toast in 350° oven until crisp (about 15 minutes).

SERVES 4–6

This is fine for a buffet. Incidentally, the toasted bread cups are better, we think, than patty shells and much easier to make.

PARTY SHRIMP CAKES

2   cups cooked, deveined shrimp
3   scallions
5–10 water chestnuts (canned)
    Rind of 1 lemon, grated
    Juice of same lemon
2   eggs, lightly beaten
¼   tsp powdered ginger
1   tsp seasoned salt
¼   tsp seasoned pepper
    Unflavored bread crumbs as desired (about 1 cup)
1   stick butter
    Flour
1   tsp ground coriander
⅛   tsp (or more) cayenne pepper

Chop finely the first 3 ingredients and combine gently with the next 7. Put this mixture in the refrigerator for at least 2 hours, or until you are ready to use it (up to 8 hours is all right).

Then melt butter gently in a heavy skillet. Dredge the shrimp mixture after patting it into cakes about the size of hamburgers in flour seasoned with ground coriander and cayenne pepper. Brown the shrimp cakes lightly for 3 to 4 minutes on each side over low heat. Turn only once.

SERVES 4

If your store has no canned water chestnuts buy a can of Chinese mixed vegetables and take out the water chestnuts. You can use the rest of the vegetables for something else.

These cakes freeze beautifully and can be made ahead and reheated for a Saturday luncheon. If you wish, you may serve them with tartar sauce, but they are very good as is!

GOLDEN SHRIMP CASSEROLE

8 slices slightly dry bread
2 cups cooked fresh shrimp (or 2 7-oz pkgs
      frozen, shelled, deveined, cooked
      shrimp)
1 3-oz can mushrooms (drained)
½ lb sharp American cheese, grated
3 eggs, beaten
½ tsp salt
½ tsp dry mustard
    Dash of paprika, salt, and pepper
2 cups milk

Trim the dry bread, butter it, and cube the slices. Put half of this in a greased baking dish, 11″ x 7″ x 1½″. Add shrimp, mushrooms, and the first quarter pound of cheese. Now put the rest of the bread and the other quarter pound of cheese on top of the casserole. Beat the eggs with the seasonings, add the milk, and pour over the casserole. Bake for about 45 minutes in a 325° oven until mixture is set.

SERVES 4–6

And somebody will always scrape the dish! This is good any time of year and needs only a crisp salad and lots of hot coffee.

MARIAN'S SHRIMP CURRY

1   1½-lb bag frozen shrimp
3   medium-sized onions, diced
1   small green pepper, diced (about ¾ cup)
¾   cup diced celery
2   cloves garlic, cut fine
2   tbsp butter
1   can grade A stewed tomatoes

Cook shrimp until tender and drain in a colander. Cook the next 4 ingredients in butter until tender but not brown. Then add the following:

2   tbsp flour blended with 2 tsp curry powder
1   tsp salt
1   rounded tbsp brown sugar
1   tsp Worcestershire sauce
    Dash of ginger

Gently stir in the tomatoes and simmer slowly until sauce is thickened and the flavors well blended. Then add the shrimp and cook over low heat, but do not boil.

SERVES 4

I first had this in Marian's lovely house in the piney woods on Cape Cod. There were crusty rolls and fresh green beans and a delicate white wine, all seasoned with good conversation about books and people. In the moonlight, with the help of Helen Beals and Marian, I managed to turn the car around with only eighths of inches between me and each tall spicy pine.

ELAINE'S FRIED SHRIMP CAKES

1   lb fresh or canned shrimp, peeled and deveined (crab meat or lobster or chicken may be substituted)
1   cup unseasoned bread crumbs
2   tbsp oil
3   scallions, finely chopped
5   water chestnuts (canned), finely chopped
1   lemon (grate rind and squeeze out juice)

2   eggs, lightly beaten
½   tsp powdered ginger
1   tsp salt
½   tsp pepper
¼   cup flour
⅛   tsp cayenne pepper
1   tsp ground coriander
1   stick butter

Dice shrimp fairly fine, then add all ingredients except last 4. Mix well and chill. Shape chilled mixture into 4 or 6 flat patties and coat lightly with flour to which coriander and cayenne have been added. Lightly brown patties in melted butter in skillet.

SERVES 4–6

These can be made into tiny balls for appetizers. They are delicious garnished with tiny tomatoes and watercress or parsley. For dinner, serve with crisp salad and crusty French bread and coffee.

PETER'S POT

1	can crab meat	1	tbsp minced onion flakes
1	can deveined shrimp	1	tbsp dried parsley flakes
1	can chunk tuna	½	cup slivered almonds (optional)
4	hard-cooked eggs		tional)
1¾	cups Minute Rice	¼	cup sweet pepper flakes
1½	cups milk	1	cup chopped celery
1½	cups mayonnaise	3	tbsp dry sherry
1	can mushroom soup		

Drain seafood. Combine with the remaining ingredients in a large greased casserole and bake, covered, at 350° for about an hour.

SERVES 8

This is fantastically good and so easy, and fits in with an emergency-shelf program. And I do love recipes where you throw everything in at once! It comes from Pudding Hill Farm in Snoqualmie, Washington, but is equally at home in our 1690 New England farmhouse.

LOBSTER

Select live lobsters that are really alive and active. Plunge head first into rapidly boiling water to cover. This is supposed to cause instant death but is one thing I cannot do. Once, when circumstances demanded it, for I was alone in the house with guests coming for lobster, I put the lobster in a brown paper bag, shut my eyes, and dropped the whole thing in the water.

There are three sizes you can use:

Chicken—about 1 pound

Select—1½ pounds

Jumbo—2½ to 3½ pounds

Or you may get a giant up to 20 pounds if you can manage it.

Put salt in the water—or use seawater if it's available. Cover the pot and let it come to a boil again; add the lobster and time it as follows:

Chicken—10 to 12 minutes
Select—15 minutes
Jumbo—20 to 25 minutes
16 to 20 pounds—45 minutes

When done, hold lobster upside down to drain out excess water, then cut the underside lengthwise with lobster shears. Remove the sand sac at the head and the intestinal vein if you can find it. Crack the claws, twist off the back portion, and pull out the slender side feelers.

Serve with pots of melted butter. Some people like a squeeze of lemon too. Or you may serve it cold with Sauce for Cold Lobster (see "Sauces and Salad Dressings").

Have plenty of paper napkins or bibs. Don't serve anything else but potato chips and white wine or coffee.

SAVORY SALMON LOAF

1	14-oz can salmon
1½	cups soft bread crumbs
¼	cup minced celery
2	tbsp minced onion
2	eggs, slightly beaten
1	can cream of mushroom soup
	Lemon slices

Combine the first 6 ingredients and pack into an 8½" x 4½" x 2½" loaf pan. It helps if you line the bottom of the pan with waxed paper. Bake at 350° until the center is firm—about 50 minutes. Remove from oven and let stand 5 minutes, then turn onto a platter and garnish with lemon slices. Serve with Mother's Sauce for Fish Loaf (see "Sauces and Salad Dressings").

SERVES 4–6

You may use canned tuna, drained if you prefer. Serve with tiny fresh or frozen peas and a green salad.

SALMON TIMBALES

1 large can salmon
3 tbsp cream
  Juice of ½ lemon
  Seasoned salt and pepper to taste
3 eggs, separated

Mash the salmon, add the cream, seasonings, lemon juice, and beaten yolks. Mix and then add the beaten whites. Bake in greased cups set in a pan of hot water about 20 minutes, or until puffed and brown on top.

SERVES 4

This is an easy dish from the pantry shelf and goes well with herb-buttered rice and tiny peas (petit pois), also from the shelf. Or have a mixed vegetable salad and hot baked frozen rolls.

LUNCHEON SPECIAL

½ cup cooked shrimp (or a 4½-oz can)
1   cup cooked Alaskan king crab (or 1 large can, drained)
½ cup each chopped celery and green pepper
¼ cup frozen diced onion
1   hard-cooked egg, chopped
   Mayonnaise to moisten well
   6 slices bread toasted on one side

Mix the first 6 ingredients and spread on the untoasted side of bread slices in a shallow baking pan. If you use canned shrimp, rinse with cold water. Top with Soufflé Topping (next page):

SOUFFLÉ TOPPING

2 eggs, separated
1 cup grated Cheddar or American cheese
Seasoned salt and pepper to taste

Beat egg whites until stiff. Beat egg yolks and seasoning. Fold in egg whites and cheese, and spread on the shrimp and crab mixture. Bake, uncovered, in a 350° oven until puffed up (about 15 minutes).

SERVES 6

Sliced chilled tomatoes add the right touch, and if you want to be fancy, ripe melon halves filled with lime ice for dessert.

STEAMED MUSSELS

2 dozen mussels per serving
Dry white wine
Water
1 pint light cream
Pinch of thyme

Steam the mussels in equal parts of white wine and water (use about a cup of liquid to a 10-quart kettle). Meanwhile, heat cream in a double boiler and add thyme. As soon as the mussels are steamed open, put them in warm bowls for serving and add some of the broth to the cream. Taste as you add so it will not be too rich for your taste. Serve the sauce in sauceboats or custard cups. Use the bottom half of the shells for scooping the sauce.
    Serve with hard rolls and a green salad.

I first ate mussels in a famous New York restaurant where they were served in big silver bowls. A delicate white wine was poured in the wineglasses, and crusty French bread was also served. Later, on Cape

*Cod, we found we could get a pailful of mussels any time from our
own beach, and with no cover charge.*

*You gather them from the rocks where they cling, being careful to
take only those that are covered with water. They must be thoroughly
scrubbed with a stiff brush and rinsed with cold water before steaming.*

GRILLED OYSTERS

3 or 4 large oysters per person (or more
    if you really love oysters)
Lemon juice
Melted butter
Egg, slightly beaten
Bread crumbs seasoned with salt and pepper

Dip the oysters in lemon juice, then in melted butter, then in the egg.
Roll in seasoned crumbs. Broil 2 minutes on each side in an ungreased
broiler. Turn once. Serve with a green vegetable and hot rolls or crusty
French garlic bread.

*I never could learn how to open raw oysters, and on Cape Cod, friends
always bring those elegant Wellfleet oysters in season. My neighbor
Ed can open them like a dream. But there is a way to manage if you
have to. Place the oysters in a shallow pan and put them in a 400°
oven for 6 to 8 minutes. When they just begin to open—watch them
carefully—take them from the oven and plunge them in a bowl of ice
(with some water in it). Leave them about 1 second and take them
out. Insert a knife at the large round edge, and you are in business.*

BROILED SCALLOPS

1 lb bay scallops
2 tbsp butter
2 tbsp cooking oil
Lemon juice
Chopped parsley
Paprika

On Cape Cod when scallops are "in" you buy them fresh, already shelled, as you do in most markets. Pat them dry on a paper towel and arrange them in heatproof individual casseroles or flat baking dishes. Melt butter and oil and pour over. Broil about 5 minutes. Sprinkle with lemon juice just before you take them out from the broiler. Sprinkle with parsley and paprika, and serve hot in the casseroles.

SERVES 4—but 2 can take care of it.

If you must settle for the big sea scallops, cut them in thirds after cooking. Slice against the grain.

CASSEROLE SCALLOPS

1½ lbs bay scallops
1½ cups crackers, crushed with
     ½ cup melted butter
3   tbsp light cream
¼   tsp seasoned salt
¼   tsp seasoned pepper
    Paprika

Arrange alternate layers of cracker crumbs and scallops in a 9" pie tin or flat casserole. Have 3 layers of crumbs and 2 of scallops. Pour the cream over the top, dust with salt, pepper, and paprika, and bake in a hot (425°) oven for 20 to 30 minutes. Don't overcook; to test them, fish one out with a fork and try it.

SERVES 4

The tiny bay scallops of Cape Cod need only broiling in butter, but this is a pleasant variation and not as rich as the deep-fat fried ones. If you should have one of those fish-shaped, shallow ceramic casseroles (someone gave me one for Christmas), use it, and garnish with sprigs of parsley or watercress. Garlic French bread is a happy accompaniment, along with fresh green salad with plenty of cucumbers.

NOTE: *The customary rule for scallops is to allow ½ pound per person. The crumbs and cream stretch this, but better double it for 6.*

BAKED TUNA CASSEROLE

1	tbsp minced onion	2	cups milk
1	tbsp minced green pepper	2	tsp chopped pimiento
¼	cup butter	2	7-oz cans tuna, drained and flaked
4	tbsp flour		Buttered bread crumbs
1	tsp salt		
½	tsp paprika		

Sauté onion and pepper in butter for about 2 minutes. Add flour and seasonings, and blend until smooth. Add milk gradually and cook until thickened, stirring constantly. Add pimiento. Mix in tuna and arrange alternate layers of tuna and crumbs in a greased casserole. Top with crumbs and bake, covered, at 375° for about 30 minutes, or until the top is brown.

SERVES 4–6

Serve with a crisp salad and hot rolls or biscuits.

TUNA FISH PIE

2 large cans tuna fish, drained and flaked
2 cups cream sauce (see recipe)
1 tsp Worcestershire sauce
1 tbsp dry sherry or dry white wine
1 tbsp chopped parsley
   Seasoned salt, pepper, and celery salt to taste
   Pastry

Combine the first 6 ingredients and pour into a buttered casserole. Top with pastry and bake at 425° until brown (about 25 minutes).

SERVES 6

You may use one of the new pastry mixes if you wish. When guests come unexpectedly, this is an easy entrée made from the supplies on your emergency shelf. Serve a tossed salad with Italian dressing, or a fresh fruit salad (orange slices, grapefruit, avocado, etc.). Bake any leftover pastry in rounds for extra helpings.

EMERGENCY-SHELF TUNA CASSEROLE

1   can Campbell's cream of mushroom soup
½   cup milk
1   7-oz can tuna, drained and flaked
1   cup green peas, cooked and drained
       (frozen or canned may be used)
1   cup crushed cheese crackers

Empty soup into a small casserole, add milk, and blend thoroughly. Add tuna, peas, and half the crackers. Stir well. Top with the rest of crackers. Bake in a moderate oven (350°) for 20 minutes.

SERVES 4

Serve with tossed salad and, for dessert, fresh fruit and coffee.

EILEEN'S ESCARGOT SPECIAL

1   stick soft butter
1   clove garlic, minced
2   tbsp minced scallions or onion
2   tbsp chopped fresh parsley
½   tsp salt
     Pepper to taste
     Few drops of lemon juice
2   dozen snails

Beat ingredients together. Place a dab in the bottom of each snail shell, next tuck the snail in, follow by more stuffing or butter on top. If you can, let them rest overnight or several hours. Bake in a hot (450°) oven for 10 minutes. Serve with crusty French bread in chunks.

SERVES 4

I do not think snails have much flavor, but served like this, you will love them. Mop up the sauce with the bread—it is the best part of the dish!

KEDGEREE

2   cups cooked rice
4   hard-cooked eggs, diced
3   tbsp chopped parsley
2   cups flaked cooked fish (canned tuna, salmon, etc.)
½   cup light cream
    Seasoned salt and pepper

Mix all ingredients and heat in a double boiler.

SERVES 6

This is an old English dish which suggests thatch-roofed cottages and country gardens, cockle shells and silver bells. If you like, you may add curry powder for a sophisticated version. When my dear neighbor Millie came for lunch recently, we had Kedgeree in individual flat casseroles. With this, we had cucumber, sweet onion, celery, carrot, and tomato salad. We decided, while eating, that the dish would be even better with additions such as pitted ripe black olives, strips of pimiento, a dash of Worcestershire sauce, and a hint of garlic. Not to mention mushrooms.

MEATS

LONDON BROIL

1 flank steak
  Meat tenderizer
1 clove garlic
  Salad oil
  Butter
  Seasoned salt and pepper

Sprinkle the steak well with tenderizer and let stand, then rub cut clove of garlic over both sides. Sprinkle with salad oil. Place in a preheated broiler about 1½ inches from the heat and broil 5 minutes on each side. Dot with butter and season well. Using your sharpest knife, cut slices diagonally across the grain.

SERVES 4

This steak has a better flavor than the most expensive cut, and, properly cooked, is a treat. If you overcook it, it will be tough.

CORNED-BEEF CASSEROLE

> 6 tbsp butter
> 2 onions chopped fine
> 1 clove garlic, minced
> 1 green pepper, seeded and cut in thin strips
> 2 regular-sized cans corned beef
> 1 tsp dry mustard
> 1 tbsp Worcestershire sauce
> 6 tbsp chopped parsley
>   Buttered crumbs
>   Grated cheese

Melt the butter in a heavy skillet and sauté the onion, garlic, and green pepper until soft. Mix with the corned beef, dry mustard, and Worcestershire sauce. Butter a casserole and put a layer of the corned-beef mixture in the bottom. Sprinkle with chopped parsley and top with remaining mixture. Sprinkle with buttered crumbs mixed with grated cheese (Parmesan or Cheddar is best). Bake in a 400° oven until brown and bubbly, 25 to 30 minutes.

SERVES 4–6

This is a shelf-magic meal, especially good for those unexpected guests. A mixed vegetable salad goes well with it.

OLIVE'S GOURMET BEEF

1	large Spanish onion, sliced	6	medium tomatoes, cut into eighths
8	medium, fresh mushrooms, sliced	¼	lb boiled ham, cut into Julienne strips
2	cloves garlic, chopped fine	18	medium black olives, sliced
	Dash of oregano	2	lbs prime sirloin, ground twice
¼	cup olive oil		
	Seasoned salt and pepper to taste		

Sauté onion, mushrooms, garlic, and oregano in oil until slightly brown. Add salt and pepper. Bring to a boil with tomatoes, then add ham. Simmer 15 minutes and add the olives.

Form beef into 4 patties and broil. To serve, spoon hot sauce over the meat.

SERVES 4

I may say this is good even if you use a more pedestrian hamburger. For a cookout you may do the beef on the grill, but keep the sauce hot in the kitchen and bring it out at the last minute. A bowl of chilled cucumber sticks, cauliflower bits, and carrot sticks goes comfortably with this, and we like crusty French bread for sopping up the sauce.

ROAST BEEF IN WINE MARINADE

3- or 4-lb top sirloin or bottom round of beef
1 pint red wine
½ tsp garlic salt or 1 tbsp minced onion
⅛ tsp thyme
1 bay leaf

4 thin slices lemon
4 thin slices onion
Seasoned salt
Drippings or butter or margarine
½ cup boiling water

Mix wine with garlic salt, thyme, bay leaf, and lemon and onion slices and pour over the roast; let stand in a cool place for 5 hours or overnight. Remove from marinade and rub roast with seasoned salt. Place in roasting pan, dot with drippings or butter, and roast, uncovered, in moderate oven (350°). When meat begins to brown, add marinade and boiling water and continue to cook until meat is tender.

SERVES 4–6

Serve with baked potatoes and a crisp salad for a hearty dinner.

RIB ROAST OF BEEF WITH YORKSHIRE PUDDING

1 4–6-lb rib roast

Wipe with a damp cloth and season with salt and pepper and mixed herbs. Tuck fine shreds of garlic and parsley in several places under the fat, and work in a few tips of celery leaves. Roast uncovered in a slow oven (300°–350°). For rare beef, allow 15–18 minutes per pound; if you use a meat thermometer, take roast out *before* the thermometer registers "Rare." For one thing, a roast will go on cooking 15 minutes after you take it out, and for another, I find the thermometer at "Rare" gives a medium-rare roast. Half an hour before the roast is done, make the Yorkshire Pudding.

YORKSHIRE PUDDING

3 well-beaten eggs
2 cups milk
1 cup flour sifted with 1 tsp seasoned salt

Mix the eggs and milk, add to flour, and beat well with rotary beater or with your mixer. Now pour off the drippings from the roasting pan, leaving about ¼ cup. Set the roast on a warm platter away from the puppies and kittens. Pour the batter in the roasting pan and increase the oven heat to 400°, or hot. Bake 30 minutes, or until pudding draws away from the edges of the pan and is golden brown on top. Serve in squares or wedges with the roast.

SERVES 4–6

This is my Aunt Minnie's recipe and was handed down in the family. Aunt Minnie said it kept your strength up, and hers was a testament, since at eighty-three she still went trout-fishing in mountain streams.

SHERRIED BEEF

2   lbs lean stewing beef
2   tbsp Lipton's onion soup mix (dry)
¼   cup sherry
1½–2 cans cream of mushroom soup (regular)
1   small can mushrooms—stems, sliced, or whole button
     Freshly ground pepper
     Smidge of garlic and seasoned salt

Place in a casserole in the order given. Cover tightly and bake about 3 hours at 350°.

SERVES 4–6

This is a delightful weekend dish when guests are to arrive by auto "whenever they can make it." You can even make it ahead and refrigerate it, covered with plastic wrap or whatever you prefer. Fine noodles go with it, and they can cook while the company settles down. A raw vegetable salad adds the right touch.

FLEMISH BEEF RAGOUT

3 lbs lean, boneless beef chuck, cubed	½ tsp thyme, crumbled
2 tbsp vegetable oil	⅛ tsp pepper
2 large onions, peeled, sliced, and separated into rings	1 bay leaf
	1 can condensed beef bouillon
1 clove garlic, minced	1 12-oz can beer
2 tsp seasoned salt	4 tbsp flour
	½ cup water

Brown the beef in oil in a heavy kettle (or Dutch oven). Remove with slotted spoon. Sauté onion rings and garlic in the same kettle until soft. Stir in the remaining ingredients except flour and water, return beef to kettle, and simmer 2 hours, or until beef is tender. Blend flour and water and stir into boiling liquid, stirring constantly until gravy thickens. Boil 1 minute. Bake at 350° for 2 hours.

SERVES 8

Serve with noodles and buttered baby carrots. This dish may be frozen prior to adding the flour and water for the gravy. We like it in mid-winter for a buffet when guests come in from walking in the snow-deep woods.

ELAINE'S STEAK AND KIDNEY PIE

1½ lbs very best beef obtainable
12 lamb kidneys, quartered
½ cup flour seasoned with salt and pepper
1 stick butter
1 large or 2 medium yellow or red onions, cubed
6 fresh mushrooms, sliced (or use canned)
1 cup hot water or 1 can consommé
¾ cup very dry sherry
Piecrust

Cube beef, add kidneys, and shake in a bag of seasoned flour. Melt butter, sauté onions and mushrooms gently, then add beef and kidneys. Turn up heat and brown slightly. Add hot water or consommé. Simmer 15 minutes and add sherry. Remove at once from heat, turn into ungreased casserole, and let cool. Top with your favorite piecrust, adding seasoned salt to batter. Or use croissant dough rolled out for piecrust top. Prick topping well and bake in 400° oven for about 45 minutes, or until crust is golden brown.

SERVES 4

Elaine says many men who say they don't like kidneys will eat their fill of this. Frozen mixed vegetables and a tossed salad go well with it.

BARBARA'S PARTY SIRLOIN TIP CASSEROLE

4 lbs beef (preferably sirloin tip), cut in 1-inch pieces
¼ cup butter
48 small, whole onions (the frozen are easy)
24 small, washed mushrooms
4 tbsp heated sherry
Salt and pepper to taste
2 tsp gravy coloring

2 tbsp tomato paste or catsup
6 tbsp flour
2 cups (1 large can) consommé
2 cups dry red wine (Burgundy)
2 bay leaves
2 tbsp parsley
2 tsp thyme
2 tsp marjoram

Sauté the beef in butter and place in a 4-quart casserole. Sauté onions and mushrooms in the same skillet. Pour sherry over the meat. Season. Add onions and mushrooms. Mix gravy coloring, tomato paste, and flour, then add consommé slowly with ½ cup of the wine. Stir, bring to a boil, and pour into casserole. Cover and bake at 250° for 3 hours. Add the remaining wine and cook another ½ hour, stirring twice.

SERVES 8 elegantly

Very nice for a buffet supper with a tossed salad. Crusty wedges of French bread are a good addition.

JOYCE BERKEY'S UNBEATABLE CASSEROLE

1   lb cubed veal
1   lb cubed lean pork
1   small onion, chopped
    Butter
1   10½-oz can cream of mush-
      room soup
1   can cream of chicken soup
1   small can of pimento, chopped
1   can mushrooms (any size)

½   lb shredded Colby cheese (or
      mild cheddar)
1   green pepper, chopped
    Salt and pepper to taste
    Buttered crumbs
1   large pkg of fine noodles,
      cooked until tender but not
      mushy

Brown meats and onion in butter, then simmer in water to barely cover until tender. Combine with remaining ingredients in large casserole. Top with the buttered crumbs. Bake at 350° for I hour.

SERVES 10

This is perfect for a party and can be made ahead and reheated. Joyce's husband is a captain in the Marine Corps and often stationed away from home while she takes care of the children and the home. This casserole is a favorite when they celebrate his homecoming with a buffet supper. You may like a huge bowl of tossed green salad and wedges of crusty garlic bread with the casserole.

NEW ENGLAND BOILED DINNER

6 lbs brisket or rump of corned beef
½ clove garlic
6 peppercorns
6 carrots
3 large yellow turnips, cut in quarters
4 small parsnips
8 small peeled onions
6 medium-sized potatoes, pared and cut in quarters
1 head cabbage, quartered

Place corned beef in cold water with garlic and peppercorns and cook slowly until tender, skimming now and then. If you use very salty corned beef, drain when it comes to a boil and use fresh water for the rest of the cooking time. Allow from 4 to 5 hours for simmering, testing tenderness with a fork. When done, remove the meat, and cook the vegetables in the stock. When the vegetables are done, return the meat to the pot and reheat.

Serve with grated fresh horseradish beaten with sour cream, or use prepared horseradish with sour cream, adding a little lemon juice.

SERVES 4–8, depending on the size of the beef

We like the beef sliced thin, not in chunks. We arrange the slices overlapping on an ironstone platter, arrange the vegetables around them with a slotted spoon, and serve the stock in an ironstone tureen (never thicken it).

We like to corn our own beef. We put it down in a crock for 36 hours, weighted down with a plate and a clean stone. The brine is 8 cups of water, 1 cup of salt, 3 tablespoons of sugar, 6 peppercorns, 1 clove of garlic, 2 bay leaves, and 2 teaspoons of mixed spices. Add ¼ teaspoon of saltpeter and ½ cup of warm water.
All I can say is, Oh, my—

OLGA'S FRICKADELLAN

2 or 3 cups leftover roast beef or lamb
4 slices light toast
1 large or 2 small onions (1 clove garlic for lamb)
1 egg
2 tbsp leftover gravy
   Milk enough to moisten to croquette consistency
   Seasoned salt and pepper
1 tsp thyme

Put the meat, toast, and onions through a meat grinder. Add remaining ingredients and mix well. Form into cone-shaped croquettes or flat patties. Fry croquettes in deep fat or pan-fry patties in butter, 5 minutes on each side. Serve on beds of watercress, or top with gravy and chopped parsley.

SERVES 4–6

Leftover beef and lamb are not dull when you make these magic croquettes of them. Serve with asparagus or baked acorn squash or minted peas. You may keep this dish hot a long time by covering it with foil and leaving it in a warm oven.

SHEPHERD'S PIE

Cubed cooked beef or lamb—whatever you
    have left over from a roast
Leftover gravy
Seasoned salt, seasoned pepper, and onion salt
Mashed potatoes enough to cover

Moisten the meat with the gravy, season, and put in a baking dish
or casserole. Cover with mashed potato and bake at 425° until
thoroughly heated and bubbly. If you have no leftover mashed potato,
use instant, but add a little extra liquid to keep it fluffy as it bakes.

SERVES 4–6

*The problem of leftover roasts is perennial. This recipe is very kind
to the budget if you have one, and is what Mama used to call rib-
sticking. If you have no gravy, use canned cream of mushroom soup.
And a few broiled mushrooms dotted on top add a touch of glamour
(mushrooms are famous for this).*

COUNTRY LAMB BAKE

6   lamb chops, shoulder cut
¼   cup flour
2   tsp seasoned salt
½   tsp seasoned pepper
1   can chicken broth, undiluted
2   tsp A-1 Sauce
2   cups onions, sliced thin
6   carrots
6   medium potatoes, sliced

Trim any extra fat from the chops and heat it in a heavy skillet. Mix flour, salt, and pepper, and coat the chops with as much of it as needed. Now brown the chops in the hot fat and remove from the skillet. Stir the rest of the seasoned flour into 2 tablespoons of pan drippings and stir until smooth, then blend in the chicken broth and steak sauce and bring to a boil, stirring constantly. Simmer about 1 minute and remove from heat. In a large casserole, layer half of the onions and carrots and then the chops. Add half of the potatoes and the rest of the onions. Overlap the rest of the potato and carrot slices. Pour the broth over all. Bake, covered, about 1½ to 2 hours. Uncover and bake about 25 minutes longer, or until fork-tender. Bake in a moderate oven (325°–350°).

SERVES 6

This is a variation of a very early country dish which used to be called the Hot Pot. I think it originated in England. Anyway, this is the way we make it, and it is an elegant Saturday night supper. The sometimes flat taste of lamb has no chance! You may add a little white wine if you wish. The cooking time varies according to how big and how thick the chops are and how thin the potato slices are, so keep an eye on it. Serve with a green salad or a platter of sliced tomatoes sprinkled with chives.

SMILEY BURNETTE'S SPICED LEG OF LAMB

        1 leg of lamb
        1 tbsp salt
        1 tbsp whole pepper
        1 tbsp allspice
        1 onion, sliced thin
        2 bay leaves
        ⅛ lb butter or margarine
        1 cup water
        ½ cup cider vinegar
        1 pint plum jam

Crush salt, pepper, allspice, and roll the onion slices in the powder. Make incisions in the lamb and insert the onion. Put the roast in the roasting pan with bay leaves, butter, and water, and sprinkle any powder left over on the top. Roast 1 hour, covered, in a moderate oven (375°), then add the vinegar and spread the plum jam over the meat. Finish roasting uncovered, basting every 10 minutes or so until the meat is tender when pierced with a fork. Remove to a warm platter while you make the gravy.

LAMB GRAVY

        Flour
        1 cup Port wine

Add flour to the pan drippings, using 2 tablespoons of flour to 2 tablespoons of drippings. Stir constantly as you add the wine. When thickened and creamy, strain and serve with the roast.

Smiley Burnette was a musician, movie actor, great gentleman, and a fine cook. When he was on the road, he carried a special portable kitchen and cooked backstage or on Western sets. This recipe will convert anyone who thinks lamb is rather dull.

CRANBERRIED LAMB SHANKS À LA INEZ

4 lamb shanks, well trimmed
1 large clove garlic
   Salt and freshly ground pepper
½ tsp savory
½ tsp crushed rosemary
   Flour
   Paprika
3 tbsp oil
1 16-oz can whole cranberry sauce (or 2 cups homemade)
¼ tsp ground ginger
½ tsp cinnamon
½ cup water
¼ tsp ground cloves
½ tsp allspice

Rub the shanks with cut side of the garlic clove and with salt, pepper, savory, and rosemary. Dredge with the flour and paprika. Heat oil in a heavy skillet and brown shanks well on all sides. Remove from pan and drain well. Place in a casserole. Heat cranberry sauce with remaining ingredients, bring to a boil, simmer 2 to 3 minutes, then pour over the lamb shanks, cover and bake 2 to 2½ hours, or until meat is fork-tender. Serve on a warm platter, dipping the sauce over the meat.

SERVES 4

Serve with fluffy white rice. Rice and lamb are happy together. Inez makes this ahead and freezes it when she has extra time. Try this on someone who says lamb isn't interesting!

GAY WINDS HAMBURG STROGANOFF

4   strips bacon, finely diced
2   onions, diced
1   green pepper, diced
1½ lbs ground chuck
½   tsp salt
¼   tsp garlic salt
     Dash of pepper
     Pinch of oregano
1   can sliced mushrooms (or ¼ lb fresh)
1   can cream of mushroom soup
½   pint sour cream

In an electric skillet cook the bacon until crisp, then push to one side of the pan. Add onions and green pepper to the bacon drippings and sauté until transparent. Add beef with seasonings. Brown the beef, but be careful not to break it up too finely. Keep it in ½″ to 1″ chunks. Add mushrooms and soup and simmer about 15 minutes. Blend in sour cream and serve at once.

SERVES 4–6

Serve with fluffy rice or fine noodles. This is elegant and can be made in a hurry. Shirley serves a good red wine with it and often Chinese cabbage.

NORWEGIAN MEAT BALLS À LA WESTA

2   lbs ground chuck
    Salt and pepper to taste
2   eggs, slightly beaten
    Cracker dust (see below)
½   cup milk
2   onions, very finely chopped
    Suet or fat
    Flour for thickening gravy
    Water as needed
    Kitchen Bouquet

Mix the meat with salt, pepper, eggs, milk, onions, and cracker dust to create desired consistency. Roll into 1″ balls. Brown in suet, remove the balls, and stir enough flour in the fat to make a smooth mixture. Add water and Kitchen Bouquet. Return the meat balls to the pan and simmer for half an hour or so.

SERVES 4–6

This was the specialty of my friend Olive's father. I suspect he rolled the crackers to make what he called the dust. For the flour 1 to 2 tablespoons may be needed.

MILLIE'S MEAT LOAF

1   lb ground chuck
1   egg, well beaten
½   cup dried bread crumbs
1½   cups milk
¾   cup diced sharp cheese
1   tsp salt
½   tsp pepper
½   tsp celery salt
¼   tsp paprika
1   medium-sized onion, chopped
1   medium-sized green pepper, chopped

Mix all ingredients well and turn into a greased loaf pan. Bake about 1 hour at 350°.

SERVES 4–5

This is a rich, moist meat loaf and is very good sliced cold the next day. If you double it, says Millie, it serves 10, but there isn't much left over! We like baked potatoes with it and sliced fresh tomatoes from Ed's garden.

BAR-B-CUED MEAT LOAF

1   lb twice-ground sirloin
½   cup rolled oats
⅔   cup evaporated milk
2   tbsp chopped onion
1   tsp seasoned salt
⅛   tsp seasoned pepper

Mix well together and bake in a loaf tin in a moderate oven (350°)
until the meat begins to draw away from the sides of the pan. This
should take about 10 minutes. Then pour over it the following mixture:

4   tsp Worcestershire sauce
2   tbsp vinegar
4   tsp white sugar
⅔   cup catsup
⅓   cup water
¼   cup minced onion

Bake half an hour longer.

SERVES 4–6

*Ruby Parks, who shared this with me, says it is their choice for a gala
outdoor supper. We like wedges of French bread for sopping any
extra sauce.*

CHRISTMAS CHOP SUEY

5 lbs onions
4 bunches celery
6 green peppers
3 lbs ground beef
  Butter
  Salt, pepper, and garlic salt to taste
2 1-lb cans bean sprouts
2 5-oz cans water chestnuts, sliced
½ lb fresh mushrooms or 2 4-oz cans
2 qts stewed tomatoes
½ tsp oregano

Cut the onions in ¼" cubes, celery in ½" slices, peppers in ¼" cubes. Place in a large kettle, barely covering with salted water. Cook for 1 hour, stirring occasionally. Meanwhile brown the beef in butter, and season with salt, pepper, and garlic salt. Set aside. Now add to the cooked vegetables the bean sprouts, water chestnuts, mushrooms, tomatoes, oregano, and salt to taste. Bring to a very slow boil, stirring occasionally. Add the beef and simmer very slowly for about ½ hour.

SERVES 6–8

This is a fine party dish, and Shirley freezes some ahead for the holiday season. An extra dividend is that she and Ginny can their own tomatoes!

Shirley and Ginny are long-time Cape friends who live on Mill Pond Road and keep the welcome mat by the kitchen door.

BOILED HAM

1 14-lb ham, ready to cook
3 bay leaves
1 medium onion, sliced
4 celery stalks with tops
1 tsp thyme

Scrub ham and place in a heavy deep kettle. Cover with cold water. Add remaining ingredients and bring to a boil. Simmer for 3 hours or until the ham is fork-tender. Let cool in the broth. Remove the skin and slice.

Very few things give a homemaker the comfortable feeling that having a cooked ham "on hand" does. Ham is just so basic, and boiled ham has countless uses—in sandwiches and casseroles, sliced thin for a buffet platter, and so on.

CRANBERRY–HAM BAKE

2 ham steaks
  Cranberry-orange relish
  Sliced orange sections

Preheat the oven to 350°. Spread one ham steak with relish and place the second steak on top. Bake about 20 minutes. Lay orange sections on top and return to the oven for 5 minutes. Spoon sauce over and serve at once.

SERVES 4

You may buy the cranberry-orange relish, or make your own as follows:

CRANBERRY-ORANGE RELISH

4 cups cranberries
1 whole orange
2 cups sugar

Grind the cranberries; seed the orange and grind it. Stir the orange and sugar into the cranberries and put in the refrigerator in covered bowls or jars. Let stand 2 days before using.

MILLIE'S HAM AND POTATO CASSEROLE

4   medium-sized potatoes
1   small onion, chopped fine
1–2 cups diced ham
1¼   cups warm milk
     Seasoned salt and pepper to taste

Grease a 2½-quart casserole. Slice the potatoes very thin and layer them with onions and ham. End with potatoes on top. Pour warm milk over the top and bake at 350° for about 1 hour.

SERVES 4

Diluted mushroom soup may be used instead of milk. Millie serves this with a jellied salad and hot rolls.

GLAZED ROAST LOIN OF PORK

1 5–6-lb pork loin
2 tsp seasoned salt
1 tsp seasoned pepper
1 tsp rosemary

Have the meat at room temperature. Wipe with a damp cloth. Place, fat-side up, on a rack in the roasting pan. Sprinkle with the seasonings and roast in a moderate oven (325°), allowing 15 minutes to the pound. If you use a meat thermometer, the roast is done when it registers 170°.

CURRANT GLAZE

⅔ cup red currant jelly
3 tbsp Port
2 tsp vinegar
1 tsp dry mustard

Mix ingredients in a pan and cook for about 10 minutes, stirring occasionally. Pour over the roast before serving.

SERVES 6

I almost never use a meat thermometer, and Connie, my daughter, said once with some dismay, "But, Mama, how can you tell when it's done?"

"By the smell," I said, "and the way it looks."

This is a nice change from the customary pork roast with apple-sauce and looks so pretty! It demands fluffy baked potatoes and a tossed salad. I have a friend who always said pork was too greasy until we had this one winter night.

JEAN'S FRUITED PORK ROAST

1   4–6-lb pork loin
½ tsp salt
½ tsp cinnamon
½ tsp allspice
½ tsp pepper
¼ tsp cloves
¼ tsp mace
6–10 pitted prunes
2   apples, cored and cut into sixths
¼ cup brandy with ¼ tsp cinnamon

Have the butcher cut along the bottom of the roast so as to make a pocket. Now mix the first 6 ingredients and rub well into the roast. Refrigerate overnight. Combine fruits, brandy, and cinnamon, and refrigerate overnight also. In the morning, poke the fruit into the pocket. If necessary hold it in with a piece of foil. Roast in a 350° or moderate oven about 3 hours or until done. If you wish, you may sprinkle with buttered crumbs during the last half hour.

SERVES 6–8, depending on the size of the roast.

Jean Lovdal serves this with creamed potatoes and a green salad, and if you think pork is dull, just try this recipe.

KAY'S GRILLED PORK CHOPS

1   large clove garlic, crushed
1   tsp thyme
1   tsp salt
½   tsp freshly ground black pepper
1   tsp lemon juice
10 center-cut pork chops, ⅜ inch or so thick

Crush garlic and mix with thyme, salt, pepper, and lemon juice. Spread on one side of each chop, stack so that both sides are in contact with the seasonings, and let stand at least an hour (if for more than 3 hours, refrigerate). Grill over charcoal about 4 inches above a hot fire until well browned on both sides. (Or brown in a heavy pan over moderate heat, turning frequently.) These chops are thin, so watch for overcooking. Test with a sharp knife if in doubt. If cooked in a pan, add ½ cup or so of water to the pan after removing the chops, scrape up the brownings, boil down, and serve as pan gravy.

SERVES 5

These are especially good with spiced apple rings (you can buy them in a glass jar). And scalloped potatoes and a plain green salad complete the dinner for a party.

PORK CHOPS AND CABBAGE

6 thick pork chops
1 large onion
1 head fresh cabbage
  Milk
  Seasoned salt, pepper, and paprika

Brown the pork chops, using a little butter if necessary. Slice the onion and add to the chops after you have turned them. Now arrange them in a greased casserole with the onion slices around them. Season well. Slice the cabbage thinly with a sharp knife and pack it tightly over the chops, filling the casserole almost to the top (it will shrink). Pour over enough milk to barely cover, add more seasoning. Bake, covered, in a moderate oven (350°) for 45 to 60 minutes, or until the chops are fork-tender.

SERVES 4–6

This recipe has been a standby at Stillmeadow since the early days and is one of those I have been asked for most often by friends and readers. So I am repeating it now. We serve it with baked potatoes. The sauce should be spooned over the potatoes. Any left over makes a good addition to a luncheon soup.

JEAN'S COUNTRY-BAKED SPARERIBS

4–6 lbs spareribs, cracked through the center and
    cut in serving pieces
2 bouillon cubes dissolved in 2 cups boiling water
¼ cup hot catsup
3 tbsp Worcestershire sauce
1 tbsp vinegar
⅛ tsp cayenne pepper
½ tsp celery salt
3 whole cloves
3 whole allspice
½ bay leaf
1 medium onion, sliced

Broil spareribs until brown on both sides, then drain off fat. Mix all other ingredients together and pour over the spareribs. Cover with foil and bake until fork-tender—about 2 hours.

SERVES 4–6 (unless I am one of them!)

When Jean calls up on a snow-deep day and asks if I want to come over to Drumlin Hill for supper, as she has spareribs in the oven, I hunt up my boots. If the road to their house is too icy, Oscar comes for me after he is through milking his pedigreed Holsteins. We eat by candlelight, and the Franklin stove sends a warm glow through the dining room.

CASSOULET FOR A HOLIDAY FEAST

1   lb white beans
3   lbs pork loin
1   ham shank
1   lb salt pork
3   lbs rolled lamb shoulder (ask
        butcher for the bones)
     Butter as needed
3   cloves garlic

Bouquet garni (1 bay leaf,
    parsley, pinch of thyme)
6   or 7 small onions
¼   lb Italian hard sausage
    Water, or water with a
        little dry wine added
    Tomato sauce
1   cup buttered bread crumbs

Soak the beans in cold water overnight. Roast the pork in a moderate oven (350°) until tender—about 2½ hours. Place the ham shank and salt pork in cold water and bring just to a boil. Now brown lamb in butter in a heavy skillet, drain the fat, and roast the lamb with its bones along with the pork until done (the lamb will take about 1½ hours—spread it with a little tomato sauce during the last ½ hour).

Drain the beans, save the water, and add enough water or water with wine to make 4 quarts. Bring to a boil, skim, add the ham shank and salt pork, garlic, and bouquet garni. Simmer covered about 1½ hours, then add the onions and Italian sausage, and simmer about an hour longer until the beans are done but not mushy.

Finally, at long last, drain the beans, add the liquor to the tomato sauce, add ham shank, sliced and trimmed of all fat, and the salt pork, diced. Slice the pork loin, lamb, and sausage. Layer the meats in a deep, heavy casserole with the beans between the layers. Skim any excess fat from the liquids, and add the liquids to the casserole. Top with buttered bread crumbs. Bake 1 hour in a moderate oven (350°).

SERVES 12

CONNIE'S QUICK VEAL CORDON BLEU

2   tbsp butter
⅓   cup fine dry bread crumbs
1   pkg green onion dip mix (there are 2 in an envelope)
¼   cup whipping cream
1   lb veal cut in thin pieces as for scaloppine
2   slices cooked ham, halved (from 5-oz pkg)
2   slices Munster cheese, halved (from 8-oz pkg)

Coat bottom and sides of a 9″ pie tin with half the butter. Sprinkle with half the crumbs. Mix onion dip and cream in a second pie tin and dip half the veal slices, one at a time, in the mixture to coat one side, then place with the coated-side down on top of the bread crumbs, slightly overlapping the slices. Top with ham and cheese. Dip remaining veal slices in the onion-and-cream mixture and place coated side up on top of ham and cheese. Sprinkle with remaining crumbs and dot with remaining butter. Bake in a hot over (400°) for 30 minutes, or until veal is tender and golden brown. Serve from the pie tin. Garnish with lemon slices and parsley if desired.

SERVES 4

When my daughter Connie suggested she would get dinner at the farm one night, I didn't think there was time enough for a gourmet meal. But in 45 minutes we sat down at the harvest table. She served hashed brown potatoes and green salad with the veal. Curt, my son-in-law, suggested that next time she should double the recipe.

ESCALOPE DE VEAU

1   lb thinly sliced veal
    Seasoned salt and pepper to taste
    Flour
4   tbsp butter and olive oil (half and half)
1   clove garlic
½   cup or more of dry white wine

Have the butcher pound the veal slices until thin and flat. Season them with salt and pepper and dredge lightly with flour. Then pound the flour into the slices with the edge of a saucer. Meanwhile heat olive oil and butter and garlic in a large skillet or electric frying pan. Brown the meat quickly on both sides. This takes 3 or 4 minutes. Remove from pan onto a warm platter. Remove garlic. Add another pat of butter to the pan and blend in 1 tablespoon of flour. Stir well, then add white wine. Scrape the pan with a wooden spoon until the sauce bubbles and comes to a boil. Pour over the veal slices.

SERVES 4

Serve with linguine or noodles tossed with butter and grated Parmesan cheese.

BAKED VEAL CUTLET

1½	lbs veal cutlets	3	tbsp water
2	tbsp flour	1	can cream of mushroom soup
½	tsp salt	1	tsp dried basil
¼	tsp pepper	⅔	cup dry white wine
2	tbsp butter		

Sprinkle meat with flour, salt, and pepper. Press in with fingers. Brown the meat in butter, then remove meat. Add water and stir, then add soup, basil, and ⅓ cup of wine. Return meat and bake in moderate (350°) oven about 45 minutes. Remove meat to a warm platter. Add remaining wine to the sauce and stir well. Season to taste with salt and pepper. Pour over meat.

SERVES 4

This is elegant, says my daughter Connie. And easy!

ZIEGEUNER (GYPSY) SCHNITZEL

6 or 7 veal cutlets (center cut of leg, medium thickness)
12–14 sliced mushrooms
2 heaping tbsp Paprika Sauce
1 tbsp dry vermouth

Place unsalted veal cutlets into hot, buttered pan and sauté on one side quickly. Turn and add to pan 2 large tablespoons of mushrooms for each cutlet, and salt. Finish sautéeing. Add Paprika Sauce, making sure it is bubbly. Add dry vermouth. Carefully remove cutlets to heated platter, stir and blend mixture remaining in the pan and spoon over.

PAPRIKA SAUCE

2 shallots
1 clove garlic, chopped
1 ample tbsp butter
2 tbsp flour
2 tbsp paprika
1 cup chicken bouillon
1 cup sour cream
 Lemon juice to taste

Sauté shallots and garlic in butter for 5 minutes over low heat. Stir in the flour and paprika smoothly. Add the stock, stirring constantly, and cook over low heat (while stirring) until thickened. Remove from heat and fold in the sour cream. Add lemon juice to taste. This sauce will keep in the refrigerator.

SERVES 4–6

This is my friend John Schwalbe's gourmet entrée. If the gypsies dine like this, I would like to be a gypsy.

KALBSHAKE (VEAL SHANK)

Have your butcher trim veal shanks at both ends, cutting through the knuckle. Wipe with a damp cloth and place in deep, oblong roasting pan large enough to accommodate the shanks comfortably. Now sliver the following vegetables:

2 large onions
4 stalks celery
1 carrot
2 cloves garlic

Sprinkle this mixture over the shanks so as to have a mound of vegetables on each shank. This will retain moisture.

Melt ¼ pound of butter and spoon it over the shanks. Sprinkle with salt and pepper and a pinch of herb butter seasoning or a pinch each of thyme and marjoram. Place in a 525° oven for 45 minutes, then turn the oven down to 350° and add 1 cup of chicken broth. Sprinkle the tops of the shanks liberally with dry vermouth. Cover and simmer for 1 hour and 15 minutes. Thicken the pan juices slightly with flour and stir well.

SERVES 6

This is exactly the way John Schwalbe copied the recipe for me, and all I can add is that, although there may be a problem getting the veal shanks in some areas, it is well worth the effort. My problem is deciding between the Kalbshake and the Gypsy Schnitzel. I start thinking it over when I know we are going to John and Marie's.

FOWL

GINNY'S BROILED CHICKEN

Chicken halves or quarters
   (allow ½ chicken for each serving)
Terriyaki sauce
Seasoned salt and pepper
Garlic salt
Pinch of marjoram

Sprinkle the chicken pieces with the sauce and seasonings and broil ½ hour if frozen, or 15 to 20 minutes if unfrozen, turning occasionally.

COMPANY CHICKEN

Cut-up chicken—12 thighs or 6 breasts
1   can cream of chicken or mushroom soup
1   cup sour cream
½   pkg dry onion soup mix

In greased oblong baking pan place chicken pieces skin side up in one layer. Mix remaining ingredients and pour over chicken. Bake at 350° for 1½ hours, or until chicken is tender. Do not cover.

SERVES 6

This makes its own gravy, and the onion soup mix gives the dish a special flavor. Curried rice and a green salad or a bowl of chilled tomato and cucumber slices go well with it.

JEAN'S CHICKEN DE LUXE WITH BROWN RICE

1   broiler or fryer cut in pieces, or 4 breasts, halved
2   tbsp olive oil
2   tbsp soy sauce
2   tbsp Worcestershire sauce
1   small clove garlic, mashed
1   tsp salt
1   tsp freshly ground pepper
1   tsp rosemary leaves, crumbled

Put the chicken in a heavy pan, bone side up. Combine all ingredients in a small bowl and brush over the chicken. Bake in a moderate oven (350°) for 15 to 20 minutes. Turn the chicken, brush with sauce again and continue baking until the chicken is fork-tender and golden brown. Serve with Brown Rice.

SERVES 4–6

BROWN RICE

1–2 cups of brown rice
    Olive oil
1   medium onion, diced
1   stalk celery, diced
1   green pepper, diced
1   chicken bouillon cube, crumbled
1   can unsweetened pineapple chunks, drained
1–2 tsp cornstarch
    Ginger
    Cloves
1   tbsp sugar

Stir rice in oil in a heavy frying pan. Add next 4 ingredients and stir around in the oil, then add water to cover. Bring to boil, cover, and simmer over low heat until just tender (not mushy). Combine pineapple chunks with white wine and cornstarch, and heat until thickened. Add mixture to rice. Sprinkle with ginger, cloves, and sugar.

Homemade bread with this meal, of course, and a tossed salad.

ELAINE'S CHICKEN FRICASSEE WITH
PARSLEY DUMPLINGS

4 chicken breasts
4 chicken thighs
1 bunch celery, diced
1 bunch carrots (young if possible)
12 small white onions
1 stick butter
3 tbsp all-purpose flour
   Thyme, rosemary, seasoned salt, and pepper to taste
1 pkg frozen baby peas

Cook chicken in salted water until tender, then remove and cool. Skin and bone chicken. Return bones and skin to broth and reduce for ½ hour on medium heat. Strain broth and cook in it the celery, carrots, and onions. Remove the vegetables and reserve broth. In a deep pot (or Dutch oven) on low heat, melt the butter (don't brown it) and cream in flour and seasonings. Add broth. Stir until velvety, then add chicken cut in bite-size pieces, and the vegetables. Simmer on very low heat until ready to serve—1 hour or more. Now cook peas separately and use to sprinkle on top when you serve. Add raw dumplings to the fricassee, cover tightly, and cook for 15 minutes. Do not peek! Serve piping hot topped with chopped fresh parsley.

PARSLEY DUMPLINGS

2 cups sifted flour
4 tsp baking powder
½ tsp salt
2 tbsp chopped parsley (or chives)
1 cup milk

Mix all ingredients except milk, then add milk gently, stirring with a dinner fork. Drop mixture in small forkfuls over the fricassee 15 minutes before serving. Keep covered.

SERVES 4

LOUISIANA CHICKEN VIN BLANC

1   2½ - to 3-lb fryer, cut in pieces
4   tbsp (½ stick) butter
6   drops Tabasco
3   large or 8 small shallots (or small
       white onions), finely chopped
1   small clove garlic, minced
     Pinch of sweet basil
½   cup white Burgundy (Chablis, vermouth, or
       white Pinot)
½   cup water
     Salt to taste

Sauté the chicken in butter to which Tabasco has been added. Remove chicken to a platter. Add shallots and garlic to the pan and simmer over low heat until soft. Add basil (if you like it) and white wine and water. Stir well. Replace the chicken, sprinkle with salt, and simmer, tightly covered, over low heat for 30 to 45 minutes, or until the chicken is fork-tender. Serve, with the gravy, on rice.

SERVES 4–6

My Louisiana friend, Gloria, who shared this with me, says her husband tells her she can throw away the chickens and let him make a meal of the gravy and rice, which is sopping good.

SCALLOPED CHICKEN

1 stewing hen (2–3 lbs)
4 stalks celery, chopped with leaves
1 pkg thin noodles (8-oz size or more)
1 can cream of mushroom soup
   Crushed potato chips

Stew the chicken and celery until the chicken is tender, then bone and cube the meat and keep separate. Cook the noodles in the broth and celery until tender, then add the cream of mushroom soup and the cubed chicken. Mix well. You may add more soup if needed to thin the mixture. Pour into 1 large or 2 small casseroles, top with potato chips, and bake for 30 minutes at 350° or until bubbling hot.

SERVES 4–6

My friend Cynthia says she likes to divide the recipe and freeze one casserole for another time. Also, she says, you may use cream of celery or chicken instead of the cream of mushroom. I like the addition of a small can of sliced or chopped canned mushrooms and a few pitted ripe olives.

COQ AU VIN

2	young chickens, disjointed	¼	tsp each thyme, rosemary, and marjoram
	Seasoned salt	1	bay leaf
	Seasoned or freshly ground pepper	1	tbsp chopped parsley
	Flour		Leaves from 1 celery stalk
2	oz butter	½	cup sliced mushrooms
⅛	lb bacon	3	oz brandy
12	tiny onions, peeled	3	cups Burgundy
2	cloves garlic, crushed		

Rub chicken pieces with salt and pepper and dredge with flour. In a heavy skillet melt butter, then add the bacon, diced. When bacon is slightly browned, remove and set aside. Brown the chicken lightly in the skillet, then add onions, crushed garlic cloves, seasonings, celery leaves, and mushrooms. Simmer about 5 minutes, then pour the brandy over and ignite. When the flame has burned out, transfer contents of the skillet to a casserole. Add the bacon and Burgundy. Cook in a moderate (325°) oven for 2 hours. If desired you may thicken the sauce with equal parts of flour and soft butter blended together. You may also add more wine if the sauce seems too thick.

SERVES 4–6

TARRAGON CHICKEN

2 broilers, cut in pieces
¼ cup fresh tarragon leaves or 2 tbsp dried
4 shallots or green onions, finely minced
1 cup dry white wine
   Melted butter
   Thinly sliced lemon

Sprinkle the chicken pieces with the tarragon and shallots and marinate an hour or so in the wine. Broil the chicken about 20 minutes or until tender, basting with melted butter and the strained marinade. Season to taste. Place the lemon slices on the chicken for the last few minutes. Serve on a hot platter garnished with freshly chopped parsley.

SERVES 4

Strain the extra marinade over the chicken just before it is done. If you do not wish to use wine, marinate in a little lemon juice and salad oil.

CHICKEN DELIGHT

4 or 6 chicken breasts, boned, skinned,
       split in two, and dredged in flour
1 small onion, sliced thin
1 small green pepper, sliced thin
2 pkgs Village Inn chicken-flavored rice
2 cans Campbell's Golden Mushroom soup
1½ cans water
   Seasoned salt and pepper

Brown the chicken breasts in half oil and half butter. Arrange in the bottom of a flat casserole. Place onion and pepper slices on top. Mix rice with soup and water and pour over. Season. Cover tightly and bake at 350° for 1½ hours.

SERVES 4–6

Bobbi Moeller says this is fine for a company dinner and easy to get ready. She is a busy homemaker but always ready to welcome people who drop in unexpectedly. She keeps chicken breasts in the freezer for emergency Chicken Delight. We like asparagus tips and a tossed salad and crusty garlic French bread with it. And a light dessert, if any.

CHICKEN LIVERS SUPREME

1   12-oz pkg noodles
    Butter as needed
½   cup milk
1   can cream of mushroom soup
½   lb fresh or frozen chicken livers, chopped coarsely
    Salt and paprika to taste
    Parmesan cheese

Cook noodles in plenty of boiling, salted water. Rinse and drain thoroughly. Toss with butter and keep warm. Combine milk and soup, then add livers and noodles. Add seasonings except the cheese. Place in buttered casserole and sprinkle cheese on top. Bake in a 350° oven about 45 minutes, or until a nice brown crust forms on top. Then if you have a chafing dish, transfer chicken livers to that and serve by candlelight.

SERVES 4–6

We find this a nice change from the usual chicken à la king. If you like, a good white wine goes well with it.

CHICKEN MARENGO

1 medium onion, sliced thin	1 cup chicken stock
½ cup olive or salad oil	2 cups Italian style tomatoes
2 frying chickens cut in quarters	16 small white onions
½ cup dry white wine	1 lb fresh mushrooms, sliced
2 cloves garlic, crushed	¼ cup butter, melted
½ tsp thyme	Juice of 1 lemon
1 bay leaf	1 cup pitted black olives
Parsley sprigs	1 jigger cognac

Sauté the sliced onion in olive oil, then remove the onion and brown the chicken pieces on all sides. Add the next 7 ingredients and simmer, covered, for about an hour, then remove chicken. Strain sauce and cook 5 minutes. Stir small onions and mushrooms in butter, and add the lemon juice. Arrange chicken in an earthenware casserole with onion-mushroom mixture and black olives. Sprinkle cognac over the top. Add the sauce and reheat in a moderate oven (350°). Garnish with chopped parsley.

SERVES 8

Serve with fluffy rice. This is not hard, it just sounds like a lot of things to do. It is better made a day ahead, and for a party buffet it cannot be equaled.

CHICKEN AND RICE DINNER

1½   cups Minute Rice
1   pkg Lipton Onion Soup
2½   cups water
      Chicken pieces
2   cans cream of mushroom soup
1   can water
      Paprika

Grease flat casserole dish. Put rice in dish, cover with dry onion soup. Add first amount of water. Wash chicken pieces (do *not* flour) and put on top, using as many pieces as you can fit in your casserole dish. Spread mushroom soup to cover chicken pieces. Pour the can of water over. Bake uncovered for 2 to 2½ hours at 350°. Sprinkle with paprika.

SERVES 4–6

This needs a big bowl of green salad and, for dessert, whatever fruit is in season.

BOWED ROOF CHICKEN SPECIAL

Chicken breast—1 to a person
Dried beef slices—3 or 4 per person
Cream of mushroom soup—1 can for
    each 3 or 4 breasts

Skin the chicken breasts. Lay thin slices of dried beef in the bottom of a greased casserole and place the chicken breasts on top. Use a casserole large enough so that the breasts are not on top of one another. Pour the cream of mushroom soup over and bake in a moderate (350°) oven until the chicken is fork-tender. Lift out carefully so there will be slices of beef on each plate.

Ruth, of the Bowed Roof, says this is their favorite chicken dish.

CHICKEN-STUFFING SCALLOP

1   8-oz pkg (3½ cups) herb-seasoned dry stuffing
3   cups cooked and cubed or canned chicken
½   cup butter or margarine
½   cup enriched flour
    Salt and pepper to taste
4   cups chicken broth, cooled
6   eggs, slightly beaten
    Pimiento–Mushroom Sauce

Prepare stuffing according to directions on the package. Spread in a 13" x 9" x 2" baking dish. Top with a layer of chicken. In a large saucepan, melt butter, then blend in flour and seasonings. Add broth, cook and stir until the mixture thickens. Stir a small amount of the hot mixture into the eggs, return to hot mixture and pour over chicken. Bake in a slow oven (325°) for 40 or 45 minutes, or until a knife inserted in the center comes out clean. Let rest 5 minutes to set, then cut in squares and serve with sauce.

PIMIENTO–MUSHROOM SAUCE

1   can cream of mushroom soup
¼   cup milk
1   cup dairy sour cream
¼   cup chopped pimiento

Combine ingredients. Heat and stir until hot.

MAKES 12 servings

This is not exactly a diet dish, but my friend Margaret Bond says it is a fine basic dish for a buffet luncheon or supper. And you can always diet tomorrow!

DUCKLING À L'ORANGE

1   5–6-lb duckling
    Seasoned salt and pepper
4   tbsp butter
2   oranges, peeled and quartered
½   cup consommé
½   cup white wine or orange juice
1   tsp cornstarch
    Water as needed

Wipe duckling with a damp cloth, rub with salt and pepper, and brown in a heavy kettle in the butter. Scrape the bitter pulp from the orange peel and cut a couple of tablespoons in thin strips. Add the peel, the orange quarters, and consommé, and cover. Simmer until the drumstick moves easily up and down (about 1½ hours). Remove duckling to a warm platter. Pour off all but ½ cup of the juices and add the wine or orange juice. Bring to a boil. Meanwhile mix the cornstarch in enough water so it will pour, add to the sauce, and stir until slightly thickened. Pour over the duckling and garnish with thin slices of orange.

SERVES 6

If you wish to simply roast the duckling, stuff the body cavity with tart, quartered apples and halved onions. Roast at 325°. Spoon extra fat from the pan as it drips down. You may make traditional gravy with the chopped, cooked giblets stirred in.

GRANDMA VON STEIN'S ROAST DUCK
WITH PFEFFERKARTOFFEL (SPICED POTATO)

2 frozen 4-lb ducklings
4 cups peeled and cubed potatoes
2 large onions, cubed
2 heaping tbsp powdered thyme
1 tsp each celery salt, seasoned salt, pepper

Thaw frozen ducklings overnight in roaster. Scald cavity in the duck-lings and try out the fat in heavy skillet at low heat. Boil potatoes for 5 minutes and sauté onions in the fat. Drain all but 2 tablespoons of fat from the skillet and add the partly cooked potatoes and seasonings. Brown potatoes lightly and stuff the ducklings with the mixture. Roast in an open, shallow pan (2 ducklings to a pan) at 375° for about 2 hours until golden brown and tender when pierced with a fork. Baste with frozen, concentrated orange juice or apple jelly for the final 15 minutes in the oven.

SERVES 4

Serve on a platter garnished with watercress and spiced whole peaches. One duckling serves 2 amply. This is a fine menu for a snowy winter night. Any green vegetable goes well with it. Elaine Von Stein says her grandma liked spiced red cabbage with it.

DUCK SUPREME

1	4–5 lb duck, cut in serving pieces
	Salt and pepper
3	tbsp flour
¾	cup chopped onion
5	carrots, cut in 1-inch pieces
¼	tsp thyme
½	bay leaf
¾	cup fine white wine
1¾	cups chicken broth (canned or fresh)
	Chopped parsley
3	or 4 white turnips, peeled and cut in pieces
3	tbsp butter
1	pkg frozen peas or 1½ cups fresh, cooked

Remove the duck fat and dice it. Heat in a heavy ovenproof skillet. Dust the duck with salt and pepper and flour and brown in the fat, then put the skillet in the oven at 450° and roast for 20 minutes. Remove from the oven and pour off most of the fat, then add onions, carrots, thyme, and bay leaf. Stir the duck pieces around and return to oven for about 5 more minutes. Reduce the heat to 400°. Add wine, chicken broth, and parsley, and mix all together. Bake 20 minutes more. Add the turnips and bake 20 minutes, or until the turnips are tender but not mushy. Keep the skillet covered (you may use foil). Now heat the butter and cook the duck liver 10 minutes, then dice. Remove duck and vegetables to a warm platter and skim the fat from the gravy and strain it. Add peas and liver to gravy, bring almost to a boil and pour over the platter.

SERVES 4

If you do not like duck liver, simply cook it and save it for the cat or puppy. Don't give it all at once, as duck liver is very rich.

CORNISH HEN ROSÉ

⅔ cup cooked rice
6   tbsp rosé wine
    Dash of pepper, allspice, and salt
½   tsp sugar
2   tbsp raisins
2   tbsp butter
2   tbsp blanched, slivered almonds
2   Cornish hens

Have the rice warm. Add wine, seasonings, sugar, and raisins. Cover and let stand 10 minutes. Melt butter, stir in almonds and brown slightly, then add to rice mixture and stuff into the hens. Roast uncovered in a 450° oven for 15 minutes. Lower heat to 350° and roast ½ hour longer, basting several times with the following:

2   tbsp rosé wine
1   tbsp butter
1   tsp lemon juice

If you want to be extra elegant, make a gravy as follows:

½   tbsp butter
½   tbsp lemon juice
4   tbsp currant jelly
    Dash of cayenne pepper
2   whole cloves
¼   cup water

Combine ingredients and simmer for 5 minutes. Strain and add ¼ cup of rosé. Mix this in with the pan juices. Thicken, if you wish, with a little cornstarch (1 teaspoon) blended with a little water.

SERVES 2–4

ROAST GOOSE

  1 goose (10 lbs)
      Seasoned salt
      Cored and quartered apples
      Celery leaves
      Stuffing—1 cup to each 1 lb of goose

Wipe goose with a damp cloth. Sprinkle the cavity with seasoned salt, then fill with apples and celery leaves. Preheat the oven to 450°. Place goose on a rack, reduce the heat at once to 350°. Allow 25 minutes to the pound. Prick in several places to let the fat run out, and pour off the fat as it accumulates. Bake the stuffing separately in a casserole, using your favorite bread stuffing, prepared commercial stuffing, or Apple and Prune Stuffing.

APPLE AND PRUNE STUFFING

  ½ lb dried prunes
  2   tbsp seedless raisins
  2   tbsp cracker crumbs
  ¼ tsp seasoned salt
  ¼ tsp sugar
  1   egg yolk, beaten
  2   medium apples, peeled, cored, diced

Pour boiling water over the prunes and raisins and let stand 5 minutes. Drain. Remove prune pits and cut the prunes in pieces. Add remaining ingredients and bake in a moderate oven (350°).

MAKES 2 cups; increase amounts as needed.

Roast goose, properly cooked, is a traditional Christmas bird. It does no harm to light some heated brandy and pour over, so the goose comes flaming to the table.

SHIRLEY'S TURKEY STUFFING

1	lb sausage meat
1	lb ground beef
1½	cans seasoned bread crumbs
1	tsp oregano
½	tsp garlic salt
1	tsp salt
	Dash of pepper
2	tbsp Terriyaki sauce
	Turkey giblets boiled until tender (reserve liquid)
4	onions
1	green pepper
4–5	stalks of celery
1–2	eggs

Brown the sausage and ground beef in a large skillet. Place the bread crumbs and seasonings in a bowl. Grind the giblets, onions, green pepper, and celery, and add to the bread crumbs. Mix well. Add the browned meat. Add enough water from the giblets to moisten well. If necessary, add a little more warm water. Blend in eggs, slightly beaten.

Shirley says that what won't fit in the turkey may be put in a greased baking dish and baked in a moderate oven (350°) about 1 hour before the bird is done. The way I feel, I would settle for the dressing even without the turkey! This is a super stuffing.

AFTER-THANKSGIVING BAKE

1   medium-sized can mushrooms, drained
2   cups or more cubed turkey
¾   cup mushroom soup, undiluted
2   cups mashed potatoes
1   cup grated Cheddar cheese
2   tbsp butter, melted
¼   cup soft bread crumbs

Mix together the mushrooms, turkey, and soup. Place in a greased 8″-square baking pan. Combine potatoes and 4 tablespoons of cheese and spread over the turkey. Pour butter over the top and sprinkle with bread crumbs and remaining cheese. Bake at 425° for about 25 minutes.

SERVES 4–6

The problem of leftover turkey can be discouraging. This is a nice change from turkey sandwiches or creamed turkey or turkey soup. Serve with a crisp salad and some more of that cranberry sauce. Have fresh fruit for dessert with a pot of coffee.

VEGETABLES

ASPARAGUS

Asparagus
Salt
Butter

Break the asparagus ends off and use them for stock some other time. Now use a heavy skillet and put enough salted water in it to barely cover the bottom. Add a dollop of butter. Bring to a boil and gently

159

lay the asparagus tips in so they do NOT touch each other. Cover and let steam for 5 minutes. Test with a fork. Add a little more water if the pan has boiled dry. Use 2 skillets if you have too much asparagus for one. The minute the fork goes in easily, take the asparagus out and place the stalks on a warm platter. Add more butter to the liquid in the skillet and pour over the stalks. Serve on toast or plain.

Asparagus is usually overcooked, with the tips nothing but mush and the stalks as limp as a rag doll. Overcooking also makes asparagus seem slimy. I feel this queen of vegetables is either delicious or not fit to eat, according to how it is cooked. My Abyssinian cat, Amber, agrees with me. She eats the tips and I eat the rest, and we make a whole meal of asparagus on toast when it is in season.

HARVARD BEETS

1 13½-oz can beets, sliced or diced, drained
½ cup sugar
½ tbsp cornstarch
½ cup vinegar

Mix sugar and cornstarch and add to vinegar. Boil together for 5 minutes. Pour over beets and let stand in a warm place for at least 30 minutes. Reheat before serving.

SERVES 4

This recipe is an old favorite and bears repeating. I remember it from my childhood. It gives beets, which are rather bland, a sparkle.

CONNIE'S KIDNEY-BEAN CASSEROLE

2 No. 2 cans kidney beans, drained
3 small onions, cut fine
½ green pepper, chopped
¼ cup chopped ham (or more)
1 small can tomato paste
1 cup red wine (Burgundy)
  Bacon strips

Mix the beans with the onions, green pepper, ham, and tomato paste. Pour the red wine over. Place in a greased casserole and lay the bacon strips on top. Bake about 30 minutes in a moderate oven (350°).

SERVES 4

This is elegant for a buffet supper. Serve with a mixed green salad and crusty garlic bread. There is never any left over. Save the juice from the beans to add to soups or stews.

BARBECUED LIMA BEANS

2	cups dried lima beans	1½	tsp chili powder
¼	lb diced salt pork	1	tsp salt
1	onion, sliced	1	can tomato soup diluted with
1	clove garlic		½ can water
¼	cup fat or drippings	⅓	cup vinegar
1½	tbsp dry mustard		Thin slices of salt pork
2	tbsp Worcestershire sauce		

Soak the beans overnight in cold water, then drain, cover with fresh water and simmer until tender with the salt pork. Drain, reserving 1½ cups of the liquid. Now brown the onion and garlic in the fat, add remaining ingredients and the liquor from the beans. Simmer 5 minutes. Place beans and sauce in a deep greased casserole, top with salt pork slices, and bake in a hot oven (375°) for about 30 minutes, adding more bean liquor as needed.

SERVES 6

This is one of the best main dishes for a buffet. Thinly sliced ham and a mixed green salad should go with it.

CALIFORNIA BAKED BABY LIMA BEANS

1   lb dried baby lima beans
2   tsp salt
¾   cup brown sugar
1   tbsp dry mustard
⅓   cup butter, melted
1   tbsp molasses
1   cup sour cream

Wash beans well and soak overnight. Drain, cover with water and 1 teaspoon of salt, and cook until tender but not mushy. Drain and rinse under hot water. Put in a lightly greased casserole. Mix sugar, mustard, 1 teaspoon salt, and butter, and pour over the beans. Stir in molasses, then add sour cream, and mix in lightly. Bake 1 hour at 350°.

SERVES 4–6

My friend Mabel says this is the best ever and not like any other recipe she ever saw anywhere. If you feel as I do about mustard, you can increase the amount. For a buffet supper for church or garden club or whatever, try taking this as your contribution. It is undeniably rich, but for a party, who cares?

CAULIFLOWER SPECIAL

1 whole head of cauliflower
4 tbsp melted butter
  Grated cheese
  Buttered bread crumbs
  Crisp crumbled bacon bits

Soak cauliflower, head down, in ice water with salt added for 15 minutes. Place the head on a rack in a deep kettle. Cover the bottom of the kettle with boiling water and cover the kettle. Steam cauliflower for 15 to 20 minutes until tender but not mushy. Drain well and place on a warm platter. Cover with the cheese, crumbs, and bacon bits. Serve surrounded with whole baby carrots or green beans. Broiled mushroom caps do no harm either.

SERVES 4–6

SHIRLEY'S CHINESE CABBAGE

1 medium head of Chinese cabbage, washed
     and cut in 1″–1½″ slices
½ lb fresh mushrooms, diced
   Butter

Place the cabbage in salted water and boil. In 20 minutes, test with a fork. When almost tender, add the mushrooms. Cook for another 7 minutes. Drain and pour melted butter over. Serve hot in warm bowls.

SERVES 4–6

The delicate flavor of Chinese cabbage is at its best in this dish. Shirley's theory is that most cooks do not appreciate some of the less usual vegetables. This is one I like best of all.

CONNECTICUT CORN PUDDING

6   strips bacon, fried until crisp
½ green pepper, diced
1   small onion, diced
2   cups corn (fresh, frozen, or canned)
½ cup soft bread crumbs
2   eggs, beaten
2   cups top milk
1   tsp salt
½ cup buttered crumbs

Drain bacon on a paper towel. Sauté pepper and onion in 2 table-spoons of the bacon drippings; add corn, bread crumbs, eggs, milk, salt, and bacon. Stir together. Pour into greased 1½-quart casserole. Top with buttered crumbs. Bake at 375° for about 40 minutes.

SERVES 6

When corn is in season and you have had enough of munching the ears, this is a happy solution. Sliced ham and tossed salad makes it a party supper.

CUCUMBERS IN SOUR CREAM

2   large cucumbers
½ tsp seasoned salt
1   tsp paprika
½ tsp sugar
1   tbsp tarragon vinegar
     Seasoned pepper to taste
6   scallions or 1 small onion
     Sour cream to cover

Slice cucumbers thin and cover with ice water for 15 minutes. Drain. Combine remaining ingredients and pour over the cucumbers just before serving.

SERVES 6

BAKED EGGPLANT

> 1 eggplant, pared
> Soft butter, enough for spreading
> Pepper, salt, grated onion, and lemon juice to taste

Cut the eggplant crosswise into ½″ slices. Spread both sides of each slice with the butter and seasonings, place them on a baking sheet and bake at 400° for about 12 minutes, turning once.

When I was growing up, eggplant was always sliced, salted, and weighted down with a flatiron until the black-purple juice came out. Then the slices were dipped in batter and fried until golden. The theory was that the juice was not good for one.

SHIRLEY'S EGGPLANT

> 2   eggs, beaten
> ¼ cup milk
> ½ tsp seasoned salt
> ½ tsp garlic salt
> ¼ tsp marjoram
>   Dash of seasoned pepper
> 2   tbsp grated cheese
> 1   medium-sized eggplant,
>   washed and sliced in ½″ rounds

Mix together all ingredients except the eggplant, then dip the eggplant slices in the batter and sauté slowly in butter in a large skillet.

SERVES 4–6

HOPPING JOHN

¼ lb bacon
½ cup Minute Rice
1   large can black-eyed peas
1   can consommé (2 cups liquid)

Dice the bacon and fry until crisp, then add to rice, peas, and consommé, and boil, uncovered, until well blended and bubbly. Stir and cover. Let stand 10 minutes.

SERVES 4

I first had this in the Virginia countryside and ate three helpings. Of course they cooked their own peas and did not use Minute Rice, but this quick-and-easy version is a favorite. Serve thinly sliced ham or beef or chicken with it and a mixed green salad. Or eat it out of soup bowls by itself.

WILLA'S CURRIED ONIONS AND RICE

3   large onions (3″ in diameter,
         if you want to measure)
1½ cups cooked rice
¾   cup evaporated or top milk
¼   tsp curry powder
     Pinch of mace
½   tsp salt (or more)
3   tbsp butter or margarine

Peel and slice onions ¼″ thick. Cook in salted water until tender, then drain. Add remaining ingredients and heat well in top of a double boiler.

SERVES 6

Serve in a casserole and dust the top with paprika. It goes well with beef, lamb, chicken, or ham. For that matter, I could make a whole meal of it by itself, any day.

HONEY-GLAZED ONIONS

12 large onions, peeled
½ cup melted butter
⅔ cup honey
⅓ cup catsup

Parboil the onions in boiling salted water until partly tender. Place in a shallow baking dish (preferably glass or ceramic). Blend the remaining ingredients and pour over the onions. Bake in a moderate oven until the onions are fork-tender and the glaze is thick and almost candied. Baste frequently.

SERVES 8–10

I am repeating this recipe since I have so many requests for it. With Thanksgiving turkey or with roast chicken, it adds just the right fillup. I have a few friends who will eat onions only this way.

BAKED POTATOES

1 potato to a person
Butter as needed

Scrub and dry the potatoes—use Idahos if you can get them. Bake 40 minutes or 1 hour in 425° oven. Rub with butter when they begin to bake. When half done, prick the skins with a fork to let the steam escape. Serve at once when done or they will shrivel. Serve with butter or cultured sour cream and chives, or with pan juices from your roast.

Potatoes wrapped in foil are not baked; they are steamed, and this is a different vegetable entirely. It is all right if you are cooking your meal on a charcoal grill simply because the foil keeps them from charring.

POTATOES ANNA

3   lbs large potatoes, pared
¾   cup butter or margarine
    Seasoned salt and pepper to taste

Slice the potatoes into thin slices and lay on paper towels. Heat the oven to 475°. Melt the butter in a saucepan, skimming the foam from the top as it heats. Pour the butter into a small dish. Discard the milky fluid at the bottom. Now heat ½ cup of the butter in a large heavy skillet over medium heat and add the potatoes, tossing them with a spatula or wooden spoon. Remove from heat and let cool to luke-warm. Heat remaining butter in a 7″ cast-iron skillet. Lay the potatoes in overlapping circles until the bottom of the skillet is completely covered, then sprinkle with salt and pepper. Arrange slices around the edge of the skillet, standing them upright. Add more layers of the slices, overlapping them, until you have used them all, adding more salt and pepper as you go. Now press potatoes down with the spatula. Set the skillet on the upper oven rack and bake about 20 minutes, then press down again. Bake about 35 minutes more and remove from the oven. Pour off excess butter. Run a knife around the edge of the skillet. Put a warm platter over the top and invert the potatoes. Gently lift the skillet off.

SERVES 8

This gives you a beautiful, crusty, golden cakelike production. It is well worth the effort. It was supposed to have been invented for some French court beauty, who probably did not have to watch the calories!

PERFECT FRENCH FRIES

Seasoned salt and pepper
1 large Long Island type of potato
per serving, or 2½ lbs for 4
Corn oil

Tear open a clean brown paper bag and sprinkle in the salt and pepper. Wash and peel the potatoes. Meanwhile heat the oil in deep-fat fryer or heavy kettle to 375°. Slice the potatoes ½″ thick, then into ½″ strips. Try to keep the sizes even. Place the strips in a frying basket and lower gently into the hot oil. Fry for 4 minutes, stirring slightly with a long fork (don't get burned). Turn the heat down slightly. Remove potatoes and let rest for 2 minutes. Then turn heat up again to 400° and gently immerse potatoes once more. After 30 seconds, lift them out and drop them in the brown paper bag. Shake a few seconds, then serve at once.

You may test the oil by tossing a small piece of potato in. The oil should bubble, fast and hard. These will not resemble the soggy, limp objects you usually get, and will lend glamour to any plate.

COUNTRY POTATO BAKE

3   cups raw potatoes cut in strips as for French fries
½   cup milk
1   tbsp butter
1   tsp seasoned salt
½   tsp seasoned pepper
½   cup finely shaved cheese
1   tbsp chopped parsley

Lay the potato strips in a greased baking dish and pour milk over them. Dot with butter and sprinkle with salt and pepper. Bake, covered, in a hot oven (400°) for 40 minutes, or until the potatoes are tender; then sprinkle with cheese and parsley, and bake 5 minutes more, or until cheese is melted and bubbly.

SERVES 4

This is a nice change from regular scalloped potatoes and goes well with sugary slices of ham and a green salad.

POTATOES À LA ELAINE

1 medium potato per person
  Cooking oil
  Salt

Scrub but do not peel the potatoes. Cut them in wedges approximately the size of half a hard-cooked egg. Dip in cooking oil and salt lightly. Place in a foil-lined shallow pan and bake at 375° for 35 to 40 minutes. Slip under the broiler to brown for 2 minutes before serving.

Elaine says Idahos are best, but any good potato will do. The men in her family simply love them, although they are not potato lovers as a rule.

SWEET-POTATO PUFFS

1 No. 202 can sweet potatoes
1 small can crushed pineapple
  Salt to taste
  Flaked cocoanut
6 miniature marshmallows

Drain and mash sweet potatoes. Drain and add pineapple. Salt to taste. Form into 6 balls. Roll in flaked cocoanut and place on a greased baking sheet. Press a marshmallow on the center of each. Bake at 375° for 20 minutes or until nicely browned.

SERVES 4

This is especially good with cold, thinly sliced ham or turkey.

LITHUANIAN POTATO ZEPPELINS

7–8 medium-sized raw potatoes
4 boiled potatoes, mashed
1 tsp salt
½ tsp pepper
2 eggs, beaten
½ lb ground beef
1 small onion, chopped
   More salt and pepper to taste

Peel and grate the raw potatoes, then strain through a cloth. Add boiled potatoes, 1 teaspoon salt, ½ teaspoon pepper, and eggs, and combine thoroughly. Pat this mixture into oblongs about the size and shape of small frankfurter rolls. On each oblong place a spoonful of meat to which chopped onion, and more salt and pepper have been added. Fold the potato mixture up around the meat. Drop into boiling salted water and boil for 20 to 25 minutes. Serve with melted butter or sour cream. You may substitute cottage cheese for the meat.

SERVES 4–6

This was a favorite at the farm across the road. Tessie, the daughter, remembers many things that happened at Stillmeadow before we came, including one murder and one suicide. Her mother was a special friend of ours and although she never managed to speak much English, and I never mastered any Lithuanian, we had long happy visits. She used to gather wild mushrooms by the sackful and dry them, and Tessie knows the right varieties too—rather a lost art nowadays.

LITHUANIAN POTATO PUDDING

10 large potatoes
1 medium onion
5 slices bacon
½ cup hot milk or evaporated milk
3 eggs, beaten
¼ tsp pepper
Salt and pepper to taste

Peel and finely grate the potatoes and onion. Cut bacon crosswise into narrow strips and fry until crisp. Pour the fat and the bacon over the potatoes. Add hot milk. Add beaten eggs one at a time, add salt and pepper. Pour into a greased pan. Bake at 400° for 15 minutes. Reduce heat to 375° and bake 45 minutes longer. Cut into squares and serve hot with sour cream.

SERVES 4–6

This is another recipe from the farm across the road. Mama Phillips (Philliponi) cooked on a big black range. She regulated the heat by how much wood she put in the stove, but Tessie uses the modern button controls. Until we began to raise our own potatoes, we always had a bushel of freshly dug potatoes as a gift—and the plump, mealy, tender vegetable did not resemble anything you get at a supermarket!

BOILED RADISHES

Young radishes
Boiling salted water
½ tsp butter, or
    cream sauce

Slice the radishes thin and cook in boiling water until just tender. If they are not small, you may peel them first. Dress with melted butter or cream sauce.

This really elevates radishes from something more than a raw nibble.

SPINACH SOUFFLÉ

2   tbsp butter or margarine
2   tbsp flour
¾   cup milk
1   tsp chopped onion
1½   cups grated Cheddar cheese
3   eggs
1½   cups cooked chopped spinach

Melt the butter and blend in the flour. Stir milk in gradually, add onion and cheese, and stir until the cheese is melted. Separate the eggs and beat the yolks. Add with the spinach to the first mixture. Beat the whites until stiff and fold in gently. Pour into a greased casserole and bake in a moderate oven (350°) for about an hour, or until a knife inserted in the center comes out clean. I usually set the casserole in a pan of hot water, since this is like a custard.

SERVES 4–6

FRIED TOMATOES WITH BACON

Ripe tomatoes, sliced thickly
Flour enough to dredge slices
Salt and pepper to taste
Bacon slices
1 cup or more top milk or half-and-half

Put enough flour in a flat pan to hold the tomato slices and stir in seasonings. If tomatoes are medium-sized, just cut them in half. Dredge them in the flour. Fry bacon slices until crisp. Remove and fry the tomatoes in the hot fat, turning just once. When they begin to brown, remove from fire and lay them on a warm platter. Now stir flour into the fat and add the milk. Stir until smooth and the gravy bubbles up. Pour over the tomatoes, top with the bacon slices and serve at once.

Use 2 tablespoons of drippings to 2 tablespoons of flour to 1 cup milk. If you allow 2 tomatoes per person, this amount of gravy is enough for 2 to 3 people. Increase the amount according to how many you are serving.

For this recipe, you have to rely on your own judgment, alas. One friend of mine always wants fried tomatoes when she comes, because she says her gravy is always stiff and lumpy. If you keep stirring and add more milk as you need it, you will have a rich, creamy sauce delicately colored with tomato juices and absolutely worthy of gourmets. Serve with toast points. True fried-tomato lovers do not want anything else, not even salad. Just more fried tomatoes, please!

TOMATOES PROVENÇALE

4 ripe tomatoes
   Seasoned salt and pepper
⅓ cup bread crumbs
1 clove garlic, minced
2 tbsp chopped scallions or leeks
4 tbsp minced parsley
3 tbsp olive oil
   Butter

Cut the tomatoes in half and scrape out the seedy parts. Sprinkle with salt and pepper and turn upside down to drain. Combine remaining ingredients except the butter and stuff the tomatoes. Put in a greased pan, dot with butter, and bake at 400° (hot) for about 15 minutes.

SERVES 4

This is especially good with baked ham or roast lamb.

SKILLET CHERRY TOMATOES

1 tbsp butter
2 small onions, peeled and diced
3 cups cherry tomatoes, stemmed
½ tsp dried basil
1 tsp sugar
1 tsp salt

Sauté onion until golden, add the tomatoes and basil, sprinkle with the sugar and salt. Continue cooking, shaking the skillet frequently. Cook about 5 minutes, or until the tomatoes are soft and juicy.

SERVES 4–6

You have a real taste treat when you try this. The cherry tomato really comes into its own.

GREEN TOMATO PIE

3	cups sliced green tomatoes
1⅓	cups sugar
3	tbsp flour
½	tsp salt
3	tbsp lemon juice
4	tsp grated lemon rind
1	recipe plain pastry
3	tbsp butter or margarine

Combine tomatoes, sugar, flour, salt, lemon juice, and rind. Pour into pastry-lined pie plate, dot with butter, add top crust. Bake for 10 minutes at 450° and then at 350° for 30 minutes or until tomatoes are tender and crust is golden.

SERVES 4–6

Serve with your favorite cheese and hot coffee. This is the answer to a surplus of green tomatoes and almost makes you wish they never did ripen!

SPINACH SUPREME

1½   cups chopped spinach
3   strips bacon, cooked and drained
2   tbsp bacon fat
2½   tbsp flour
      Milk, as needed (see below)
4   green onions, chopped
1   garlic clove
      Grated Parmesan cheese

Cook spinach in a little more water than usual, then drain well and save liquid. Blend bacon fat and flour over low heat, then add milk and spinach liquid—1 or 2 cups to make a medium cream sauce. Add chopped onion. Rub garlic clove on the stirring spoon and stir the sauce again. Fold in the spinach gently. Heat well but do not boil. Add crumbled bacon. Serve with a sprinkling of Parmesan cheese.

SERVES 4–6

This is a way to persuade non-spinach-eaters that they love it! It is also a help if you have a garden and spinach, spinach, spinach. My theory is that most people who hate spinach just get it boiled to death and served plain.

HONEY-BAKED ACORN SQUASH

3   acorn squash
½   cup honey
½   cup butter
1   tsp ground cloves
2   tsp soy sauce
1   tbsp water

Cut the squash in half lengthwise and scrape out seeds. Place cut sides down in a baking pan and pour in boiling water about ½" deep. Bake at 375° for 35 minutes, or until tender. Meanwhile combine remaining ingredients and heat over low heat until butter melts. Turn squash right side up. Cut each half lengthwise and spoon the liquid over. Bake 15 minutes longer, basting again. Place squash on a warm platter and serve the remaining glaze with it to spoon over.

SERVES 6

I am a squash addict and have a problem deciding which kind I like best and which way I favor for cooking. But this appeals to non-squash-eaters, so we have it often. I also bake it and leave the halves whole and fill them with brown sugar, butter, and salt, and let them stay briefly in the oven to melt the brown sugar. A third easy way is to fill the centers with creamed spinach, sprinkle cheese over, and bake an extra 15 minutes. Packaged, frozen creamed spinach is good for this—especially if you have already served it at another meal and have just a few dabs left over.

STUFFED ZUCCHINI

6   medium-sized zucchini
1   tsp seasoned salt
2   eggs, lightly beaten
1½   cups whole kernel corn, drained
2   tbsp chopped green onion
2   oz sharp cheese, shredded

Cook zucchini in boiling water for about 7 minutes. Drain, cut off the ends and cut the zucchini in half lengthwise. Scoop out the centers, leaving the shell intact. Dice the scooped-out squash and drain. Sprinkle shells and squash with salt. Combine eggs, corn, green onion, and seasoned salt, and add to diced squash. Spoon into the shells and bake, uncovered, in a 350° oven for about 25 minutes. Sprinkle cheese over tops and bake until cheese melts nicely.

SERVES 6

Try this sometime on a guest who announces that he or she just can't stand any kind of squash! We like it with thin slices of cooked ham or rare roast beef and hot rolls.

SALADS

AVOCADO SALAD

2 avocados, peeled, halved, and rubbed through a sieve
2 tbsp lemon juice
1 envelope gelatin in ¼ cup cold water, dissolved over hot water
1 16-oz can mandarin orange segments
1 large can unsweetened pineapple chunks
2 envelopes unflavored gelatin in ½ cup cold water, dissolved over
    hot water
    Chicory, watercress, or other salad greens

Add lemon juice to the sieved avocado, then add the first envelope of
dissolved gelatin. Line a 1½-quart oiled and chilled mold with the

181

avocado mixture. (You may have to do this ⅓ at a time, turning the mold on one side and chilling after each time.) Now drain the orange segments and pineapple. Reserve the juice. Soften the second 2 envelopes of gelatin. Add 1½ cups of juice. Chill. When gelatin begins to set, fold in orange and pineapple, and fill the lined mold. Chill until firm. Unmold on a round platter covered with greens.

SERVES 4–6

Serve with sour cream dressing, mayonnaise, or French dressing. This is a party luncheon dish of Jean Lovdal's. She serves it with a light white wine, hot rolls, and cold sliced chicken.

FOUR-BEAN SALAD

1   can green beans, drained
1   can golden wax beans, drained
1   can garbanzos (or chick peas), drained
1   can red kidney beans, drained
1   large onion, thinly sliced
1   large green pepper, thinly sliced
½   cup vinegar (wine vinegar preferably)
½   cup sugar (go easy on this)
½   cup olive oil
    Seasoned salt and pepper to taste

Drain beans, and mix with onion and pepper in a large bowl. Blend the vinegar, sugar, and olive oil together and pour over. Let stand overnight in the refrigerator. Before serving, add the salt and pepper.

SERVES 4–6

This is probably the most popular winter salad at Stillmeadow. I use the finely slivered green beans.

WINTER BEAN SALAD

3	tbsp finely chopped onion	3	tbsp wine vinegar
3	cups chopped celery	¾	cup olive oil
3	15½-oz cans kidney beans, drained	1½	tsp dried red pepper, crushed
2	tbsp chopped parsley	¼	tsp dried thyme
⅓	cup lemon juice	¾	tsp dried oregano leaves
		¾	tsp seasoned salt

Combine onion, celery, beans and parsley. Blend remaining ingredients and fold into beans. Marinate in refrigerator for several hours.

MAKES about 12 servings

This is a hearty and satisfying salad for a buffet supper, summer or winter. Save the drained bean liquor and add to soups or gravies. Never waste it!

KAY'S CHICK PEA SALAD

3   tbsp minced sweet onion
1   clove garlic, crushed
¾   tsp fresh or dried basil (you may like more)
¾   tsp oregano
½   cup salad oil (I like olive)
2   tbsp wine vinegar
¾   tsp salt
½   tsp black pepper
1   tsp Dijon style mustard
2   20-oz cans chick peas

Combine all ingredients except the chick peas. Heat peas to boiling in their own liquid, drain well, and mix immediately with the other ingredients. Cool. Just before serving, correct seasoning to taste and add:

2 tbsp mayonnaise
3 tbsp fresh minced parsley
2 or 3 minced scallions

SERVES 4–6

This is fine in place of a potato salad or as an appetizer with meats and cheeses. Add 2 more teaspoons of mustard if you like it as well as I do.

CARROT SALAD

3 or 4 good-sized carrots, shredded on the coarse
  side of the shredder
Celery, shredded to equal the amount of carrots
Walnuts, broken in pieces, about a handful
Seasoned salt and pepper

Toss all ingredients together. Mix mayonnaise with some chili sauce to taste and add to the bowl. Add more seasoning as needed. Serve on a platter edged with watercress.

SERVES 4–6

This is a fine winter salad and gives those inevitable carrots a lift.

GLADYS GLOVER'S CHERRY SALAD

1   No. 303 can dark cherries
1   No. 2 can crushed pineapple
1   large pkg dark cherry Jell-O
1   small bottle Coca-Cola
½   cup chopped pecans
1   cup chopped celery hearts
2   8-oz pkgs cream cheese

Drain juice from fruits and bring 1½ cups to a boil. Dissolve the Jell-O in this. Remove from fire, add Coca-Cola, and chill in the refrigerator. When it starts to chill and set, add fruit, nuts, celery hearts, and cream cheese, cut in small bits.

SERVES 4–6

This is rich enough for a dessert if you don't need a salad! It is better made the day before and put in the refrigerator overnight.

CHICKEN SALAD

2 cups cold cubed chicken
1 cup unsweetened pineapple chunks, drained
1 cup walnut halves or pieces
1 cup celery, cut in ½" pieces
  Mayonnaise
  Curry powder to taste
  Seasoned salt and pepper

Mix together in a bowl and turn out on a platter rimmed with watercress or parsley.

SERVES 4–6

BELGIAN ENDIVE SALAD

2 stalks Belgian endive
1 ripe avocado
1 small or ½ large cucumber
  Boston lettuce or romaine
  Roquefort dressing

Cut the endive stalks in half, peel the avocado, remove seed, and slice lengthwise into thirds. Peel the cucumber and quarter lengthwise. On a bed of lettuce or romaine alternate the slices of vegetables and avocado. Pour Roquefort dressing over.

SERVES 4–6

HILLCROFT GELATIN MOLD

2 pkgs of your favorite flavor of gelatin
12 oz boiling water
12 oz fruit juice (to blend with the flavor you choose for the gelatin)
8 oz sour cream

Blend gelatin and hot water, add juice and mix. Blend in sour cream with a wire whisk. Chill in a ring mold or bowl.

Serve with fish or chicken salad in the center of the ring for luncheon, with fruit or sherbet for summer desserts, or on lettuce as a dinner salad.

SERVES 6

Bobbie, Jill's daughter, says she uses cranberry Jell-O and pineapple or orange juice and adds fresh chopped cranberries for a tart, fruity salad. I find this especially good with baked ham.

Another favorite is lime Jell-O with pineapple juice, but you can invent many variations. This salad can be made ahead.

LENTIL SALAD

1 pkg lentils
¼ cup salad oil
⅛ cup lemon juice (or to taste)
1 large onion, finely chopped
⅓ cup chopped parsley
1 tsp salt
   Freshly ground pepper to taste

Soak the lentils in warm water for 2 hours. Skin the lentils by gently rubbing them between your palms under slightly running water. After most of the skins have been removed, drain, and cook in slightly salted water for 15 minutes, or until tender but not soft. Use a generous amount of water, as lentils expand. When tender, remove from heat, strain off excess liquid, and place in a shallow pan for quick cooling. Meanwhile, prepare dressing of oil and lemon juice and add while the lentils are still slightly warm. Add onion and parsley and season with salt and pepper to taste. Mix lightly but thoroughly with fingers, lifting from the bottom. Allow to finish cooling at room temperature, then refrigerate.

SERVES 4–6

Serve in small bowls as salad. This is a top favorite at the Inn of the Golden Ox, and is a delightful change from the invariable tossed green salad!

LIME RING

2   3-oz pkgs lime-flavored gelatin
2   cups boiling water
1½ cups cold water
½   cup cider vinegar
1   cup chopped green cabbage
½   cucumber slices (do not peel but cut very thin)
½   cup minced green pepper

Dissolve gelatin in boiling water, then stir in cold water and vinegar. Chill until partly set. Stir in cabbage, cucumber, and green pepper. Pour into a lightly oiled 6-cup ring mold. Chill until firm. Unmold and fill center with shrimp, lobster, or tuna salad. Garnish with pimiento strips and parsley. Dot center with black olives if you have some on hand.

SERVES 8

One more make-ahead dish for a buffet luncheon or supper on the terrace. If it is midsummer, serve iced tea with fresh mint leaves. (See Beverages)

MACARONI SALAD

1   8-oz pkg elbow macaroni
1   can pimiento, drained and cut fine
1   cup diced green pepper
1   tbsp minced onion—or more if you like
½   cup mayonnaise
½   cup sour cream
1   tsp seasoned salt
½   tsp seasoned pepper
    Greens (optional)
    Paprika
    Ripe olives (optional)

Cook the macaroni until tender but not mushy. Rinse in cold water and drain. Mix in a bowl with pimiento and green pepper and onion. Blend the mayonnaise with sour cream and add seasonings. Gently stir into the macaroni. Chill several hours or overnight. Serve in a large bowl or on a platter garnished with romaine, watercress, parsley, or whatever you wish. Dust with paprika. I like to add pitted ripe black olives too.

MAKES about 3 quarts

When I go to one of those gourmet buffet dinners with all kinds of elegant crepes and lobster and shrimp dishes, I may as well admit I fill my own plate with macaroni salad and home-baked beans.

TOMATO GELATIN SALAD

1	pkg lemon Jell-O
1	small can tomato sauce
1½	cups boiling water
2	tbsp white vinegar
1	tsp Worcestershire sauce
⅛	tsp salt
⅛	tsp seasoned pepper
½	cup chopped sweet pickle
½	cup chopped olives
1	cup chopped celery
	Dash of garlic salt
	Dash of onion salt
	Dash of sugar

Mix boiling water with Jell-O and add tomato sauce, vinegar, Worcestershire sauce, then add remaining ingredients. Turn into a ring mold or pan and chill in the refrigerator until set.

SERVES 4–5

This goes well with sliced ham or cold sliced chicken or—well, almost anything. Also you can make it the day before and you are not tossing salad at the last minute. Dorothy White, who gave it to me, says it is good to have on hand any time of year.

DRUMLIN HILL HOT POTATO SALAD

2–3	lbs potatoes	4	tsp sugar
1	tsp salt	2	tsp salt
¼	cup olive oil or safflower oil	¼	tsp pepper
2	tbsp vinegar	¼	cup vinegar
	Salt and pepper	½	cup water
4	or 5 slices bacon	¼	cup minced onion
½	cup minced onion	2	tbsp snipped parsley
1½	tsp flour	1	tsp celery seeds

Cook potatoes in jackets in boiling salted water until tender but not mushy. Peel when cool enough to handle, and cut into ½" cubes. Place in a 4-quart bowl and pour over the olive or safflower oil, vinegar, and salt and pepper to taste. Mix gently and set aside.

Meanwhile sauté bacon until crisp, remove from pan. Add first amount of onion and sauté till tender. In a bowl mix the flour, sugar, salt, and pepper, stir in the vinegar and water until smooth, and add to onion and bacon fat in the pan (if bacon is very fat, pour off a little before adding). Simmer until thickened slightly. Pour this hot over the potatoes, then add second amount of minced onion, parsley, and celery seeds.

Mix gently and serve warm; or you may do this a day ahead and heat through in a moderate oven in an ovenproof platter covered with foil.

SERVES 4–6

This is true Scandinavian potato salad and is the best in the world, as far as I am concerned.

The Lovdal farm overlooks a beautiful glacial drumlin that rolls gently to the sky. Even with 50 head of cattle, 30 milking and 20 young stock for replacement, the Lovdals find time to enjoy the view.

ZEE CLAIBORNE'S SHRIMP SALAD

2	lbs shrimp, cooked and shelled	1	tbsp wine vinegar
1	lemon, sliced very thin	3	small garlic cloves, mashed
1	red onion, sliced thin	1	bay leaf
2	tbsp pimiento	1	tsp salt
12	black olives, pitted		Dash of cayenne pepper
½	cup fresh lemon juice	1	tbsp dry mustard
¼	cup olive oil		Black pepper to taste

Put first 5 ingredients in a bowl. Blend remaining ingredients for the dressing and pour over the shrimp. Marinate overnight in the refrigerator. Stir occasionally.

SERVES 12

OLIVE'S SPINACH SALAD SUPREME

1	pkg raw spinach
3	hard-cooked eggs, chopped
¼	lb bacon, broiled and broken in small pieces
	Salt and pepper to taste
	Green Goddess salad dressing

Wash and stem spinach and break up the leaves, then add egg and bacon bits and seasoning. Add the dressing and toss.

SERVES 4–6—but 3 will finish it!

This is a hearty and masterful salad which non-spinach-eaters invariably love. The amount of dressing you use depends on your own taste. We like the salad just crisp but not dry.

ELAINE'S SALAD BAR

Wedges of iceberg lettuce with Roquefort or Thousand Island dressing.

Stuffed cherry tomatoes. Stuff with crab meat, shrimp, chicken, cottage cheese, or tuna and egg salad. Serve on Boston or Bibb lettuce, topped with mayonnaise.

Ham salad on a bed of crisp cucumber slices, garnished generously with 2″ lengths of celery stuffed with chive cheese.

Thin-sliced iced cucumbers in sour-cream sauce with generous amounts of chive and dill added.

Old-fashioned fresh fruit salad with plenty of strawberries on top. Blueberries are nice with this.

Canned grapefruit sections with alternating slices of avocado which have been marinated in garlic dressing.

Philadelphia cream cheese squares (cubes) on split bananas topped with chopped pecans and served on watercress. (*I loathe bananas, says Elaine.*)

Slices of Jerusalem artichoke marinated in garlic dressing. Serve on Bibb lettuce.

Marinated beans: lima, kidney, string, Italian green. Marinate in Italian dressing and mix together. Serve in lettuce cups garnished with chopped parsley, watercress, and pimiento.

Avocado stuffed with marinated knob celery cut in tiny pieces and topped with chopped parsley.

PEG'S WINTER SALAD

1 can tomatoes with onion
1 box lemon Jell-O
　Celery, chopped fine
　Green olives, sliced
　Mayonnaise
　Horseradish

Mash the tomatoes and heat, then add Jell-0. When cooled, add rest of the vegetables. Serve with mayonnaise to which you have added a little horseradish.

SERVES 4

SAUCES AND
SALAD DRESSINGS

BLUEBERRY SAUCE

¾ cup water
¼ cup sugar
1 tbsp lemon juice
1 tsp cornstarch dissolved in 1 tbsp water
1 cup blueberries

Cook the syrup 1 minute, then add the blueberries and cook about 30 seconds more. It should just come to a boil, but don't overcook it.

Spoon it over vanilla ice cream or custard pudding or pound cake slices. If you can pick your own blueberries, so much the better.

197

BÉCHAMEL SAUCE

2   cups milk
4   tbsp butter
½   small onion, minced
4   tbsp flour

Bring the milk to a boil in the top of a double boiler over boiling water. Melt butter in a skillet and simmer the onion until golden. Stir the flour in gradually and slowly add the hot milk and stir until smooth and creamy. Simmer about 15 minutes until the flour is cooked, stirring occasionally. Strain through a fine sieve and serve.

If you are serving it with fish, you may use half fish stock and half milk. Also if you wish a more elegant sauce, add 1 beaten egg yolk and reheat but do not boil.

Connie, my daughter, says I could cook with only two utensils, my double boiler and the Dutch oven, and she does have a point. I actually wear out a couple of double boilers a year by starting something and then letting the water boil away in the bottom, so I advise peeking frequently.

CREAM SAUCE

2	tbsp butter
1½–2	tbsp flour
1	cup warm milk
	Seasonings

Melt butter and stir in flour until smooth. Add milk gradually, stirring constantly with a wire whisk until thick, creamy and smooth. Keep the heat low. Season to taste.

I suppose the word "basic" might be defined as cream sauce. You may add almost anything from chopped hard-cooked eggs (Egg Cream Sauce), onion flakes, or bay leaves to Worcestershire sauce and chopped spinach (Florentine Sauce). Or you may add 1 cup of finely chopped poached oysters and 3 tablespoons of chopped parsley and have an elegant sauce for any fish.

The secret of a good cream sauce is to prevent or smooth out lumps by stirring and to cook until the sauce has lost that raw, floury taste.

HORSERADISH SAUCE

¾ cup consommé
½ cup dry white wine
½ cup grated fresh horseradish
1 cup sour cream
3 tbsp very fine bread crumbs
1 tsp dry mustard
   Seasoned salt and pepper to taste
1 egg yolk (optional)

Mix the consommé, wine, and horseradish with the sour cream. Simmer about 15 minutes. Add crumbs and seasonings. For a thick sauce, add beaten egg yolk mixed with a little of the sour cream and stir constantly until thick and smooth.

This is a prime favorite for those who like old-fashioned boiled brisket of beef or a platter of cold meat. My Jill used to enjoy it on a piece of fresh, warm bread!

MOTHER'S SAUCE FOR FISH LOAF

1 cup milk
1 tbsp cornstarch
1 tbsp butter
2 tbsp catsup or chili sauce
   Dash of red pepper
1 egg

Heat milk to a boil and thicken with cornstarch. Add the butter, catsup, and pepper, then add the egg, and boil about 1 minute. Pour over the fish loaf when it comes from the mold.

My mother was a gourmet cook but seldom used any recipes; she just cooked. She did write this down for me when I was a bride facing the uncharted wilderness of a kitchen. Because, she said, I couldn't go wrong with it!

SAUCE FOR COLD LOBSTER

Sieve the tomalley from the lobster. Blend with mayonnaise (home-made if possible). Add 1 teaspoon of Dijon mustard, chopped parsley, chopped chives, a few capers, a dash of lemon juice, and pepper.

Fill the cavities of the split lobster. If you want to gild the lily, as it were, dribble chopped hard-cooked egg on the lobster's tail, and lay lemon wedges around the platter.

Some like it hot, some like it cold, as the saying goes, and I like it both ways equally. But at least, when it is cold, you won't have hot butter all over everything.

WESTERN VIEW MUSTARD SAUCE

2   egg yolks
½   cup sugar
2   tbsp dry mustard
1   tsp seasoned salt
1   large can evaporated milk or 1 pint light cream
½   cup vinegar

Beat the egg yolks and stir in the sugar, mustard, and salt. Add just a little of the milk to make a smooth mixture. Meanwhile heat the rest of the milk in the top of the double boiler, but do not let it boil. When it is hot, stir the egg mixture in slowly, stirring constantly until it thickens. Then remove from the fire and stir the vinegar in slowly. Return to the stove and cook about 5 minutes, or until the sauce is thick and creamy. Watch it carefully so it will not curdle. Serve hot.

If I had to settle for just one sauce, it would be this. Serve with baked ham. It is also good the next day cold with a platter of cold meats. Good for sandwiches too. Or added to salad dressings. We serve it in a good-sized bowl, just ladled out generously. I think evaporated milk is better than cream for this, as it is less apt to curdle.

SAUCE RANCHERO

2 tbsp salad oil
3 large tomatoes, skinned, seeded, and chopped
1 small onion, minced
   Seasoned salt to taste
1 tsp sugar
2 tbsp seeded and chopped chili peppers
1 medium green pepper, seeded and diced

Heat the oil in a heavy saucepan, add tomatoes and onion, and cook slowly for about 25 minutes, stirring frequently. When the mixture is a nice purée, add the remaining ingredients. Serve over broiled or baked hamburgers—hot or cold as you wish.

Peeling and seeding is not my favorite occupation, but this is a good sauce, so it's worth it. If you dip the tomatoes briefly in boiling water, the skins come off easily.

COLD MEAT SAUCE

3   tbsp currant jelly
1½   tsp grated lemon rind
1½   tsp wine vinegar
½   tsp dry mustard
3   tbsp sherry
3   tbsp red wine

Blend well. Serve with cold meat.

I have friends who always remark when they do a roast that they get tired of having it cold. I happen to love thinly sliced cold meat, whether it is ham, beef, or lamb. But I think a nice juicy sauce gives an added touch and if you garnish the platter with watercress sprigs, parsley, or tomato wedges, you will enjoy every bite. If you have no watercress or parsley, tuck a few crisp lettuce leaves around the edge.

DE LUXE HAMBURGER SAUCE

½ cup soft butter
2   tbsp prepared mustard (preferably Dijon)
½ clove garlic, crushed
     Salt and pepper to taste
¼ lb blue cheese put through sieve

Cream the butter with the mustard, garlic, salt and pepper, and add to the cheese. Spoon over hot broiled hamburgers.

If you have a blender you may use it. This is my favorite hamburger sauce. I find a little blue cheese goes a long way by itself, as I prefer the Bries, mild Cheddars, and so forth. But this way, I keep spooning more on.

D'ANN'S BARBECUE SAUCE

1   cube butter, melted
½ cup olive oil
½ cup catsup
1   tbsp prepared mustard
1   tsp Worcestershire sauce
     Juice of ½ lemon
1   tbsp grated onion—or more if you wish
1   tbsp garlic powder or 1 garlic clove
     Seasoned salt and pepper to taste

Shake well. Use as a marinade or basting sauce. This is delicious for meat done on the outdoor grill—but not bad on the broiler either.

TOMATO SAUCE

2 tbsp butter
2 tbsp flour
1 cup tomato juice or cooked, strained tomatoes
    Seasoned salt and pepper to taste

Melt the butter in a skillet, blend in the flour, and cook until smooth.
Add the tomato and seasonings and cook over low heat until thickened.

MAKES 1 cup

*This is a basic tomato sauce. You may add mushrooms, chives, parsley
—or chopped onion and pepper sautéed in butter or garlic or
Worcestershire sauce—all depending on what you want to use it for.*

SHIRLEY'S QUICK SPAGHETTI SAUCE

3 small onions, finely diced
1 quart Gino's Italian spaghetti sauce with mushrooms
1 large can Italian plum tomatoes, put through food mill to remove
    seeds
1 6-oz can tomato paste
1 tsp garlic salt
1 tbsp Italian seasoning
1 small can mushrooms, drained, or ½ lb fresh mushrooms, diced

Sauté onions until transparent. Mix remaining ingredients and simmer
on low heat in a heavy kettle about 2 hours, stirring occasionally.

SERVES 4–6

*This isn't exactly quick, but is easier than taking a whole day to make
spaghetti sauce, which Shirley often does when she has time. With 3
grandchildren popping in and out and always a houseful of weekend
guests, time is sometimes a problem.*

VICKY'S SPAGHETTI MEAT SAUCE

1   large can Italian tomatoes
1   medium-sized can tomato sauce
2   small cans tomato paste
1   onion, chopped
1   clove garlic, minced
    Chopped parsley
    Oregano to taste
2   bay leaves
    Worcestershire sauce as desired
    Seasoned salt and pepper to taste
½   lb raw ground beef

Blend the first 3 ingredients, then add the rest and simmer for an hour or so with the lid off, stirring frequently. Simmer another hour, covered, stirring frequently. Let rest in the refrigerator several hours before using (rest yourself too from all that stirring and hovering). Serve over cooked spaghetti. HOT!

MAKES enough sauce for 8–10 servings

When you serve a smaller number of guests, freeze any leftover sauce for future use. You may add a can of mushrooms later. Vicky says she may use 4 tablespoons of olive oil if she feels like it. Spaghetti sauce is one of the most personal of recipes. You taste and add the seasonings as you go along. I am lavish with the Worcestershire sauce. When cooking the spaghetti, be sure you do not turn it into a soggy mass. It should be firm, or what they call "al dente." Be careful not to let the strands get broken up, says Vicky. Half the fun is trying to twist them on a soup spoon or tablespoon.

Serve with crusty French bread (here go the calories) and a green salad. No dessert, please.

BASIC FRENCH DRESSING

1½   cups imported olive oil
½   cup wine vinegar
2   tsp seasoned salt
1   tsp sugar
½   tsp seasoned pepper or freshly ground black pepper
1   tsp paprika

Combine all ingredients in a jar with a top and shake until blended. Store in a cool place and shake just before pouring over the salad.

MAKES 2 cups

This is the true French dressing. When you ask for it in a restaurant you get something that does not resemble it but is a creamy thick pink sauce. The nearest approach to it in the commercial dressings is called oil and vinegar. But if you make your own—and do use pure olive oil—you have something you will dip a piece of bread in and sop up after the salad is gone.

MAYONNAISE

HAND-BEATEN MAYONNAISE

½ tsp mustard
½ tsp sugar
⅓ tsp salt
   Dash of cayenne pepper
1 egg yolk
2 tbsp vinegar or lemon juice
¾ cup olive oil

Sift the dry ingredients into a bowl. Add egg yolk and beat well. Then add, stirring constantly, 1 tablespoon of the vinegar or lemon juice, drop by drop, beating with a wooden spoon. Then gradually add the oil, beating constantly, a teaspoon at a time. When it thickens add the remaining vinegar or lemon juice, stirring it in carefully. If the mayonnaise is too thick, add 1 teaspoon more vinegar or lemon juice.

MAKES about 1¼ cups

Have all ingredients at room temperature before you begin, or the sauce may curdle. If you have added the oil too rapidly and the mayonnaise does begin to curdle, put an extra egg yolk in another bowl and gradually beat in the mayonnaise.

BLENDER MAYONNAISE

Place in the electric blender the following:

> 1   egg
> 1   tsp dry mustard
> 1   tsp seasoned salt
>   Dash of cayenne pepper
> 1   tsp sugar
> ¼   cup olive oil

Cover and blend until thoroughly mixed, then, with the blender still running, remove cover and slowly add alternately:

> ½   cup olive oil
> 3   tbsp lemon juice

Then add:

> ½   cup more olive oil

Blend until creamy and smooth.

I think the hand-beaten mayonnaise is especially delectable, but the blender is easier. I had one sad experience making the blender recipe when the blender motor went on a binge and heated up so that the mayonnaise was cooked.

There are many ways to vary mayonnaise. For fruit salads, for instance, you may like to beat ⅓ cup cream until stiff and fold in 1 cup mayonnaise. Or you may add curry powder to taste, which is excellent with shrimp salads. Or for a vegetable salad you will find the following a nice change:

TOMATO MAYONNAISE

1 cup mayonnaise
2 tbsp tomato paste
½ tbsp lemon juice
½ tsp Worcestershire sauce
1 tsp sugar

Blend all ingredients gently and serve on a crisp fresh vegetable salad.

DRESSING FOR GREEN SALAD

1 clove garlic, minced
  Handful of chopped fresh basil
  Handful of chopped parsley
  Freshly ground pepper (or seasoned pepper)
  Seasoned salt
  Lemon juice and olive oil (4 parts oil to 1 part lemon juice)

Mix the first 5 ingredients in a bowl. Add oil and lemon juice (or wine vinegar) worked together with a pestle. Just before serving, add the greens and vegetables of your choice.

This recipe comes from Drumlin Hill; Jean likes romaine, Boston lettuce, chicory, endive, avocado, tomatoes, and black olives for the salad itself. So do I!

BLUE CHEESE SALAD DRESSING

1   pint Kraft mayonnaise
½ lb blue cheese
½ pint light cream
¼ cup milk
⅓ cup French dressing

Blend ingredients together.

This is a satisfying dressing for mixed vegetable salads or with fresh, crisp, garden lettuce.

HEAVENLY SALAD DRESSING

¼   cup mild vinegar
¾   cup pineapple juice
⅓   stick butter
1   tsp prepared mustard
1   tsp flour
¼   cup sugar
½   tsp salt
4–5 egg yolks

Heat liquids with butter and mustard until butter melts. Mix flour, sugar, and salt. Beat the egg yolks and stir in sugar mixture. Stir liquid in. Cook slowly until thick, stirring often.

This is an unusual and excellent dressing. For a party fruit salad, you may fold in some whipped cream.

RÉMOULADE SAUCE

1   cup mayonnaise
1   cup catsup
½   onion, grated
1   tsp prepared mustard
1   tsp Worcestershire sauce
¾   tsp seasoned salt
     A good dash of Tabasco

Beat all ingredients together with a wire whisk. Chill in the refrigerator. This sauce keeps as long as mayonnaise. Use for salad dressing or as a shrimp dip or in deviled eggs. You may thin it, if necessary, with sour cream or more mayonnaise.

JOYCE BERKEY'S SALAD DRESSING

1   qt real mayonnaise
3   cups buttermilk
2   level tsp salt
2   tsp onion powder
½   tsp garlic powder
2   tbsp chopped fresh parsley
2   tsp Accent
¾   tsp black pepper

Mix all ingredients well.

MAKES 1¾ quarts

Joyce says that her husband, after two years in Japan as a captain in the Marine Corps, was thankful to get back to home cooking; and this dressing is his favorite. She also uses it as a sauce over vegetables, or a dip, or over baked potatoes. She adds a little more garlic and onion powder for their own taste and sometimes thins it with a little more buttermilk.

CHOCOLATE SAUCE

3   squares bitter chocolate
⅓   cup boiling water
1   cup sugar
3   tbsp corn syrup
     Butter the size of a walnut
1   tsp vanilla
1   can evaporated milk, undiluted

Melt the chocolate in the top of a double boiler over boiling water. Add the ⅓ cup boiling water to the chocolate and stir well. Add the sugar and syrup and keep stirring. Then boil over direct heat for 4 or 5 minutes, and stir in butter and vanilla. Finally, stir in the evaporated milk and boil 1 minute.

MAKES about 2 cups

Serve this sauce on ice cream, pudding, or plain cake. This will keep in the refrigerator several weeks and may be reheated just before serving.

HARD SAUCE

⅓   cup butter
1   cup 3-X confectioner's sugar
1   tsp brandy

Have the butter at room temperature but not runny. Cream it with the confectioner's sugar, using a wooden spoon. When it is smooth add the brandy and blend it in.

MAKES about 1 cup

This is the traditional topping for Christmas plum puddings, but my children like it on unfrosted cakes just out of the oven. It is served cold in a chilled bowl on the hot pudding or cake, and then it melts slowly.

SPONGE CAKE SAUCE

2 egg yolks, beaten
   Grated rind of ½ lemon
   Juice of ½ lemon
½ cup fresh orange juice
⅓ cup sugar
   Pinch of salt
2 egg whites, beaten stiff
1 tsp vanilla

Mix in a heavy saucepan the first 6 ingredients. Cook in the top of a double boiler over boiling water until thick. Then gradually add to the egg whites. Let cool and add the vanilla.

MAKES about 1 cup

This is also good on baked custard, or even on hot waffles!

MAPLE SUGAR SAUCE

1 cup maple sugar
½ cup light cream
1 tsp vanilla

Boil the maple sugar with the cream until it forms a soft ball when you take out a teaspoonful and let it cool. Remove from heat and beat 1 minute, then add vanilla.

MAKES 1 cup

If you have a candy thermometer, the temperature will be right at 232 degrees. If not, do as I do, and poke the spoonful around with your finger. This sauce is not only elegant on pancakes or waffles but on French toast or custard or vanilla ice cream.

BUTTERSCOTCH SAUCE

½ cup brown sugar
½ cup light corn syrup
½ tsp salt
2   tbsp butter
1   tsp vanilla

Cook the brown sugar and syrup about 10 minutes, then add the remaining ingredients and stir well.

MAKES 1 cup

This is an excellent way to make plain vanilla ice cream more interesting. Or pour it over leftover baked custards or puddings or unfrosted cake.

FUDGE SAUCE

2   oz unsweetened chocolate
¾ cup sugar
½ tsp salt
1   tbsp cornstarch
½ cup light corn syrup
½ cup top milk
2   tbsp butter
2   tsp brandy or vanilla

Mix chocolate, sugar, salt, and cornstarch in the top part of your double boiler, then add the syrup and milk and cook about 15 minutes over boiling water, stirring until thick and creamy. Remove from heat and add the butter. Cool slightly and add brandy or vanilla. Serve on ice cream.

BREADS

WHITE BREAD

4 pkgs yeast
1 cup lukewarm water
2 cups milk
4 tbsp butter (you may use half
    Crisco, etc.)
2 tbsp sugar

4 tsp salt
2 cups water
12–14 cups unbleached flour
    Melted butter as desired

Dissolve yeast in the lukewarm water. Scald milk and add to it the butter, sugar, salt, and the 2 cups water. When lukewarm, add dissolved yeast. Gradually add flour to make a medium-soft dough. Knead

215

10 minutes until smooth and elastic. Put in greased bowl. Cover. Let rise until double in bulk (1½ hours). Knead 2 minutes and let rise again until double (30 minutes). Form into 4 balls and rest 10 minutes. Place in greased pans, 9″ x 5″ x 3″. Let rise until the dough is rounded above the edges of the pans (40 or 50 minutes). Brush tops with a feather dipped in melted butter. Bake at 400° for 30 or 40 minutes. Turn out on a rack. Brush tops again with butter, cover with a towel, and let cool.

If you don't have a nice feather on hand, use a pastry brush or just dribble the butter over. This recipe sounds like a lot of work, but you can always rest while the dough is resting and rising. Or you can polish the copper. For a perfect picnic you need a loaf of this bread, some cheeses, and a bottle of wine or a thermos of coffee. Fresh peaches or juicy pears or spicy purple grapes add a final touch. And think how easy it is! All you have to do is make that bread.

JEAN'S CHEESE BREAD

1	cup milk
2	tbsp sugar
2	tsp salt
2	tbsp shortening
6¾	cups flour
½	pound Cheddar cheese
3	pkgs yeast
½	cup warm water
1	cup warm water

Scald milk, stir in sugar, salt, and shortening, and let cool to lukewarm. Stir in 2 cups of the flour and beat until smooth. Grate the cheese coarsely over the batter. Dissolve yeast in ½ cup of warm water and stir into cheese mixture. Stir in 1 cup of water and add 4 cups of flour and stir until smooth. Sprinkle some of the remaining flour on a mixing board, then turn out dough. Knead until smooth and elastic, using more flour as needed to keep from sticking. This takes 10 to 20 minutes. Place in well-greased bowl, turning to grease all sides. Cover and let rise in warm place until doubled in size—about 45 to 60 minutes. Punch down dough and knead in the bowl until satiny. Form into loaves and bake at 400° until done. Turn out on wire rack to cool. The time depends on the size of the loaves you make, so test with the usual straw.

Jean Lovdal serves this warm from the oven as a dinner bread, but toasted for breakfast it can do no harm. Fine for luncheon too!

ANADAMA BREAD

    ½   cup cornmeal
    2   tbsp shortening
    ½   cup molasses
    3   tsp salt
    2   cups boiling water
    2   yeast cakes
      Flour to make stiff (about 6 cups)

Combine the first 4 ingredients and pour the boiling water over. Let cool until lukewarm, then crumble the yeast in and stir until well blended. Gradually add the flour and knead lightly. Put in a greased bowl in a warm place and let rise until double in bulk. Knead again and divide the dough into 2 parts. Place in 2 greased bread pans and let rise again until almost double. Bake in a moderate oven (375°) until the bread pulls away from the sides of the pans—45 minutes to an hour—and the top is nicely brown.

I am repeating this recipe because I have so much mail from unhappy readers who simply CANNOT find their copy and must have it at once. There are a number of legends as to how this bread got its name— it's a very old recipe—but I do not believe any of them, especially about the husband who said, "Anna, damn her," etc. In any case, it freezes well if you can keep everyone from gobbling it up!

CRANBERRY NUT BREAD

2   cups sifted flour
2   tsp baking powder
½   tsp salt
1   tsp baking soda
¼   cup butter
1   cup sugar
1   egg
1   tbsp grated orange rind
½   cup chopped nuts
¼   cup chopped citron
½   cup fresh orange juice
1½   cups fresh cranberries

Sift together flour, baking powder, and salt. Add soda to butter and mix well. Blend in sugar and beat in egg. Stir in orange rind, nuts, and citron. Add flour mixture alternately with the orange juice. Put cranberries through a food chopper, using the coarse blade. Stir into dough. Turn into well-greased and lightly floured 9″ x 5″ x 3″ loaf pan and bake at 350° for about 1 hour and 20 minutes, or until that familiar straw inserted comes out clean.

This is excellent as a tea bread, and we all know by now that cranberries are simply stuffed with vitamins.

DILL CASSEROLE BREAD

1   pkg active dry yeast (or compressed yeast)
½   cup warm water
1   cup creamed cottage cheese
2   tbsp sugar
1   tbsp minced onion
1   tbsp butter
2   tsp dill seed
1   tsp seasoned salt
½   tsp baking soda
1   egg, unbeaten
2¼ or 2½ cups flour

Sprinkle dry yeast on warm water (or crumble compressed yeast in). Heat the cottage cheese to lukewarm. Combine with sugar, onion, butter, dill, salt, soda, and egg. Add the flour to make a stiff dough, beating well after each addition. Cover and let rise in a warm place (85° or 90°) until it has doubled. This takes about an hour. Now stir down the dough and turn into a well-greased, 1½-quart, round 8″ casserole. (You may use a loaf pan if you wish.) Let rise again in a warm place for 30 to 40 minutes. Bake in a moderate (350°) oven until golden brown, about 40 to 50 minutes. Brush with butter, sprinkle with salt.

MAKES a 1-pound loaf

My friend Viola gave me this and added, "Very very good. You'll love it." She couldn't have been more right.

PEG'S IRISH SODA BREAD

1   cup white flour
2   cups stone-ground whole wheat flour
½   cup dark brown sugar (or you may use honey)
½   tsp salt
1½   tsp baking soda, dissolved in
            2 cups buttermilk

Combine first 4 dry ingredients. Stir the soda and buttermilk well. Make a well in the center of the dry ingredients and add the buttermilk mixture. Bake in 2 small, greased loaf pans for about 45 minutes in a 350° oven. Just before removing from the oven, rub a stick of butter over the tops. You may add 1 cup of floured raisins or dates or chopped prunes if you wish.

SUPPER HERB BREAD

1   pkg active dry yeast
¼   cup warm water
¾   cup milk, scalded
2   tbsp sugar
1½   tsp salt
2   tbsp shortening
1   egg, beaten
½   tsp nutmeg
1   tsp ground sage
2   tsp celery seed
3–3½ cups sifted enriched flour

Soften the yeast in the warm water. Combine hot milk, sugar, salt, and shortening, and cool to lukewarm. Add yeast and mix well. Add egg and herbs and 2 cups of the flour. Beat until smooth. Add remaining flour or enough to make a moderately soft dough. Knead on a lightly floured surface until smooth and elastic (takes about 8 minutes). Place in a greased bowl, turning once to grease the surface of the dough. Cover. Let rise in a warm place until double in bulk (about 1½ hours). Punch down. Cover and let rest 10 to 15 minutes, then shape in a round loaf. Place in greased 8″ or 9″ pie plate. Cover and let loaf rise in warm place until double (45 to 50 minutes). Bake in a hot oven (400°) for 35 minutes or until it draws away from the sides of the tin and is golden on top.

The friend who shared this says her Army husband asks for it for lunch when he can get home.

OATMEAL BREAD

> 2 cups boiling water
> 1 cup rolled oats
> 2 tbsp shortening
> ½ cup dark molasses
> 2 tsp salt
> 1 pkg yeast
> ½ cup lukewarm water
> 5–6 cups unbleached flour

Pour the boiling water over the oats, then add the shortening, molasses, and salt. Cool to lukewarm. Dissolve the yeast in the warm water and add to the oatmeal mixture, then gradually add flour until stiff. Turn out on a floured board and knead until smooth and elastic. Turn into a greased bowl. Cover and let rise in a warm place until double in bulk. Shape into two loaves and place in greased loaf pans. Cover again and let rise until double. Bake at 350° (moderate oven) about 50 minutes or until brown. Turn out on racks and let cool. Brush with butter while cooling.

On the subject of bread, Jean Lovdal says simply, "I like to make it, and we like homemade bread." In these days, commercial bread usually contains additives to make it keep longer; it is also expensive. One good way to trim the budget is to make your own and enjoy bread as Mama used to make it.

RUTH ANN'S PUMPKIN BREAD

2⅔	cups sugar	1½	tsp salt
⅔	cup shortening	2	tsp baking soda
4	eggs, beaten	1	tsp cinnamon
1	1-lb can pumpkin	½	tsp cloves
⅔	cup water	⅔	cup chopped walnuts
3⅓	cups sifted flour	⅔	cup chopped dates
½	tsp baking powder		

Cream together sugar and shortening till light and fluffy. Stir in eggs, pumpkin, and water. Sift together all dry ingredients and add gradually to pumpkin mixture. Add nuts and dates and blend well. Turn batter into 2 greased 9″ x 5″ x 3″ loaf pans. Bake at 350° for 1 hour and 15 minutes.

MAKES 2 loaves

This is Hickory Hill's favorite and deserves to be.

SAUSAGE BREAD

Buy frozen rolls, let them thaw. Roll out as many as you want into circles. Melt butter and add powdered garlic to taste and spread on the rolls. Crumble up sausage in the same frying pan you used for the butter. Cook, then drain thoroughly and crumble finely. Sprinkle this on the rolls, covering them well. Roll the circles up, pinch the ends together and let rise. Bake in a 375° oven about 10 minutes.

You will need about ¼ stick of butter and ½ pound of sausage for 8 rolls. Specific measurements are difficult with this recipe, but you can use your own judgment!

I sent this recipe in for a column in Family Circle, *and the testing kitchen tried it out. The staff members ate every crumb and said one word—"Delicious."*

POLLY JOHNSON'S WHOLE WHEAT BREAD

2 cups milk
¼ cup margarine
1 egg
½ cup brown sugar
1½ tsp salt
2 pkgs dry yeast
3–4 cups white unbleached flour
3 cups whole wheat flour

Combine milk and margarine in a saucepan and heat until lukewarm. Pour into a mixing bowl. Add egg, sugar, salt, yeast, and 2 cups of white unbleached flour. Beat for 2 minutes with electric beater. Add the whole wheat flour and stir by hand. Gradually add the balance of the white flour until the dough no longer sticks to the sides of the bowl. Place dough on a floured board. Knead for 8 to 10 minutes. Let rise in a greased bowl until double in bulk (1 to 1½ hours). Punch down. Divide in half and place in 2 greased bread pans. Let rise again until double in bulk (1 hour). Bake in a preheated oven (375°) for 40 to 50 minutes.

Polly and Hugh Johnson have a house in Wellfleet, overlooking the magical expanse of the salt marsh, laced with silver streams. One could sit all day and watch the mystery of the marsh, but Polly finds everyone who comes in is always hungry and she likes to have freshly baked bread on hand! She says for added nutrition for 1 of the 3 to 4 cups of white unbleached flour, you may use: 6 tablespoons of powdered milk, 2 tablespoons of wheat germ, 6 tablespoons of soy flour.

WHOLE WHEAT BREAD

1   pkg dried yeast
½   cup lukewarm water
2½   cups milk, scalded
¼   cup honey
1   tbsp salt
½   cup brewer's yeast
3   tbsp vegetable oil (safflower)
6–8 cups whole wheat flour

Dissolve the dried yeast in the water. Combine milk, honey, salt, and brewer's yeast. Mix well. Add dissolved yeast mixture, oil, and 3 cups of the flour. Beat well (5 minutes), or until bubbles rise to the surface. Add enough of the remaining flour to make soft but pliable dough. Turn out on board and let rest 10 minutes, then knead until elastic and smooth. Place in a greased bowl. Cover. Let rise until double, punch down and let rise again. Divide dough into 3 parts. Let rest 5 minutes. Shape into 3 loaves and place in greased pans. Let rise 1 hour or until double. Bake 15 minutes in a 385° oven. Lower heat to 350° and bake for 35 to 40 minutes. Turn out on rack to cool.

If you wish a soft crust, brush the loaves with butter when done.

My dear neighbor, who makes this often, says that kneading bread dough gives her a feeling of being related to something basic. When she brings a warm, fragrant loaf to the dinner table on a breadboard and we cut our own thick slices, I feel related to the pleasure of happy eating!

POLLY'S QUICK WHOLE WHEAT BREAD

1 cup whole wheat flour
1 cup white unbleached flour
2 tsp baking powder
1 tsp salt
½ cup brown sugar

Mix and blend well, then add the following:

1 cup milk
1 egg
2 tbsp melted butter
½ cup nutmeats, chopped,
   or chopped dates or orange peel

Beat thoroughly. Spoon into buttered loaf pan 9″ x 5″. Bake at 350° for about 40 minutes.

When the Johnsons come for weekends, Polly finds time to make this while Hugh is clamming!

STILL COVE POPOVERS

1 cup flour
1 cup milk
2 medium-sized eggs
1 tsp salt

Blend all ingredients well with a whisk or fork, but never mind if there are a few lumps! Fill greased custard cups ¾ full and set them on a cookie sheet. This amount is enough for 6 cups. Turn oven on at 450° and bake 30 minutes. *Do not preheat the oven in this instance.* Do not open the oven door, no matter how nervous you get. After 30 minutes, you may take a look, and prick the popovers lightly with a two-tined fork. Leave in the oven for 5 more minutes.

DEEP-FRIED HUSH PUPPIES

1   tbsp flour
1   cup fine white cornmeal
¾   tsp seasoned salt
2   tsp baking powder
1   medium onion, minced or grated
1   egg
6   tbsp top milk

Mix dry ingredients, then add onion and egg and beat well. Add milk and beat batter smooth. Drop from a tablespoon into 2 inches of bubbling hot fat (380°), dropping from the side of the spoon. Fry until golden brown, then dip out with slotted spoon. Serve sizzling hot with fish or chicken or barbecued meats.

MAKES 24 Hush Puppies

LILLIAN'S PITTER PATTERS

1   egg
⅔   cup white sugar
⅔   cup brown sugar
½   cup shortening
½   cup dark molasses
2   cups thick sour milk or buttermilk
2   cups white flour
2   cups graham flour
½   cup hot water with 1 tsp salt and
        2 tsp baking soda stirred in
⅔   cup raisins or chopped nuts

Cream together first 4 ingredients, then add molasses, milk, and both flours. Mix well, then add hot water with the salt and baking soda. Fold in raisins or nuts. Drop by dessert spoonfuls on a greased cookie sheet and bake about 20 minutes, as you would drop cookies. Serve with fresh sweet butter for a delicious hot bread. Any leftover dough may be baked in a loaf pan at 350° for about 1 hour, and you have brown bread.

MAKES 12–15

Lillian invented this one rainy day when she was out of bread and twelve hungry folks, she says, were right there. The children asked what it was, and she said, "I guess it's Pitter Patters." She says graham flour is a must, as whole wheat is too fine.

SALLY LUNN GEMS

1	egg
2	tbsp melted butter or margarine
2	tbsp sugar
1	cup milk
2	cups flour
1½	tsp baking powder

Beat egg and add butter or margarine, sugar, and milk. Blend in the flour sifted with the baking powder. Pour into greased muffin tins and bake in a hot oven (375° or 400°) until the tops are delicate brown and the edges draw away from the pan.

SERVES 4–6

I have no idea who Sally Lunn was, as this is a very old recipe from my childhood. I like to think of her using cast-iron muffin pans (which can't be beat) and wearing a starched and ruffled apron.

FRENCH TOAST

⅔–1 cup milk
2   eggs, slightly beaten
½   tsp salt
8   slices bread

Add milk to eggs and salt. Dip the slices of bread in and let them soak up the mixture. Fry on a hot, well-buttered griddle. You will need a whole stick of butter. Turn only once.

SERVES 4

You may serve this sprinkled with cinnamon and sugar or with maple syrup. Once in a while when the moon is blue and dieting is deadly, try a festive breakfast of French toast with crisp broiled bacon and coffee. Don't bother about the calories.

BLUEBERRY MUFFINS

1   cup milk
2   tbsp melted shortening
1   egg, well beaten
1¾   cups flour
3   tsp baking powder
½   tsp salt
4   tbsp sugar
1   cup blueberries dredged in ¼ cup flour

Combine milk, shortening and egg. Sift flour with baking powder and salt and add it with the sugar. Stir lightly and add the blueberries, folding them in gently. Drop by spoonfuls into buttered muffin tins. Bake about 25 minutes at 450°. They will be delicately brown on top and begin to draw away from the sides of the tin when done.

SERVES 4 comfortably or 6 skimpily

DESSERTS

APPLE DESSERT

1   cup sifted flour
1   cup sugar
1   tsp cinnamon
1   tsp soda
½ tsp salt
1   egg, well beaten
5   medium apples, peeled and cut in thin pieces
1   cup pecans, coarsely broken

Sift flour, measure, resift with sugar, cinnamon, soda, and salt. Add egg and mix as well as possible. Add apples and nuts. Stir with a

229

wooden spoon or fork until the juice from the apples has just moistened the mixture. Place in a greased baking pan 10″ x 13″. Bake in a moderate oven (375°) for about 30 minutes, or until the apples are tender.

SERVES 6–8

This is a good alternative to apple pie, and hungry guests are sure to take a second helping.

CHERRIES JUBILEE

   1   large can black cherries (about 2 cups)
   1   tbsp sugar
   1   tbsp cornstarch
   1   cup cherry juice
   ½   cup brandy

Drain the cherries, reserving the juice. Mix sugar and cornstarch and gradually add the juice. Cook over low heat about 5 minutes, then add the cherries. Warm the brandy, pour it over the cherries, and ignite it. Spoon the juice in the pan over the cherries and serve the dish flaming.

SERVES 6

You may serve this over vanilla ice cream if you wish. It took me some time practicing before I learned to have the brandy warm enough to ignite! We like to serve this in the chafing dish as a special dessert.

CONNECTICUT BLUEBERRY BUCKLE

¼ cup butter or margarine
¾ cup sugar
1 egg
2 cups sifted flour
2 tsp baking powder
½ tsp salt
½ cup milk
2 cups fresh blueberries

Cream butter, beat in sugar, add egg, and beat well. Then add sifted dry ingredients alternately with milk, beating until smooth. Fold berries in lightly. Sprinkle with Crumb Topping. Bake in a greased 9″ x 9″ x 2″ pan at 375° for about 35 minutes.

CRUMB TOPPING

¼ cup soft butter
½ tsp cinnamon
⅓ cup sugar
⅓ cup flour

Blend all ingredients together.

SERVES 4–6

When blueberries are ripe, this is a nice change from the inevitable blueberry muffins.

QUICK FRUIT COBBLER

½ stick butter, cut in squares
½ cup flour, sifted
½ cup sugar
1   tsp baking powder
½ cup milk
   Fresh fruit or berries

Dot bottom of ungreased casserole or pan with the butter squares. Mix flour, sugar, baking powder, and milk together. Pour over butter. Spoon fruit over all, allowing spaces for dough to bubble up. Bake in 350° oven for 30 to 35 minutes, or until golden brown on top. Especially good with peaches.

SERVES 4

STUFFED PEACHES

6   large medium-ripe peaches, skinned
      and with pits removed
½ cup grated almonds
2–4 tbsp sugar
2   tbsp grated orange rind
½ cup sherry

Fill the center of the peaches with a mixture of the almonds, sugar, and orange rind. Place peaches in a baking dish and pour the sherry over. (If peaches are underripe, sprinkle a little additional sugar over.) Bake about 20 minutes at 350°.

STUFFED PEARS

For pears, use grated walnuts, sugar, and grated lemon rind, and, if desired, bits of candied ginger. Don't forget to peel and core the pears carefully.

SERVES 4–6

OLD-FASHIONED APPLESAUCE BARS

½	cup butter
¾	cup sugar
1	egg
½	cup thick applesauce
1	tsp vanilla
1¼	cups unsifted flour
½	tsp soda
½	tsp salt
1	tsp cinnamon
¼	tsp nutmeg
⅛	tsp cloves
½	cup chopped walnuts
½	cup golden raisins

Cream butter and sugar. Add egg and beat well. Add applesauce and vanilla, and blend. Sift flour, soda, salt, and spices. Add to creamed mixture and blend well. Stir in nuts and raisins. Spread in a greased and flowered pan 13" x 9" x 2". The batter will be stiff. Bake in a 350° oven about 25 minutes. Cool slightly. Dust with confectioner's sugar.

MAKES 30 bars 3" x 1".

These are from Mabel's kitchen. She says she sometimes uses light brown sugar, omits the cloves, and adds 1 teaspoon of instant coffee. The cookie bars stay fresh in a tight container and also pack well.

LEE'S NEVER-FAIL CHOCOLATE CUPCAKES

1   egg
½   cup cocoa
½   cup shortening
1½   cups flour, sifted
½   cup buttermilk
1   tsp vanilla
1   tsp baking soda
1   cup sugar
½   cup hot water
½   tsp salt

Place in a bowl in the order given and do not mix until the last ingredient has been added. Bake in a moderate oven (350°) in a greased muffin tin. Bake about 25 minutes, or slightly longer if your tin has large cups.

MAKES 1 dozen large cupcakes

Lee says it is important to have all the ingredients at room temperature, particularly the shortening. You may use oil for shortening if you wish.

JEAN'S LEMON SOURS

¾   cup flour, sifted
⅓   cup butter
2   eggs
1   cup light brown sugar
½   cup nutmeats
¾   cup cocoanut (from a package)
⅛   tsp baking powder
⅔   cup confectioner's sugar
2   tbsp lemon juice
        Grated rind of 1 lemon

Mix flour and butter to fine crumbs and pat into 8″ x 8″ or 10″ x 12″ pan. Bake 10 minutes at 350°. Meanwhile beat eggs slightly, add brown sugar, nuts, cocoanut, and baking powder. Pour over baked crust. Return to oven and bake about 20 minutes. While still hot, brush with confectioner's sugar, lemon juice and rind, which have been mixed together. Cut into bars in the pan while still slightly warm. Then freeze before removing from the pan.

MAKES 2 dozen or more

These freeze well and are fine for afternoon tea or a coffee party.

YANKEE FRUIT SQUARES

2	cups water
2	cups sugar
1	cup raisins
1	cup dates
1	cup figs
4	cups flour, sifted
2	tsp soda
2	tsp cinnamon
½	tsp each cloves, nutmeg, salt
1	cup nutmeats

Boil together the first 5 ingredients in a heavy saucepan for about 5 minutes. Cool. Add all remaining ingredients. Mix well. Spread dough to 1″ thickness. Bake in a large (10″ x 13″) pan in a 350° oven until done. Cut in squares while hot.

Makes 25 or more

These keep well in a covered crock and freeze beautifully. Jean says they also mail well, and with two sons in the Peace Corps, finding foods that can withstand mailing is one of her problems.

MILLIE'S BROWNIES

½ cup shortening
2 oz chocolate
¾ cup flour
½ tsp baking powder
¾ tsp salt
2 eggs
1 cup sugar
1 tsp vanilla
1 cup nuts, coarsely ground or chopped
2 tbsp corn syrup

Melt shortening and chocolate over hot water. Cool. Sift flour with baking powder and salt. Beat eggs until light. Add sugar, then chocolate mixture, and blend. Add flour, vanilla, nuts, and corn syrup, and mix well. Bake in an 8″-square pan, well greased at 350° (moderate oven) for 30 to 35 minutes.

MAKES 16 brownies

There are brownies and brownies. They can be stiff and crusty or grainy. These are moist and rich and keep well—if they have a chance.

MARGOT'S SAND TARTS

½   cup butter or margarine
3   heaping tsp powdered sugar
1¼ cups flour, sifted
1   tsp vanilla
1   cup ground pecans (run through the meat chopper)
    Granulated sugar
    Pecan halves or glazed cherries

Cream butter, add sugar, and beat well. Add flour, vanilla, then ground pecans. Form small balls, roll them in granulated sugar, flatten on a cookie sheet with a fork and press half a pecan or glazed cherry in the center of each. Bake 10 to 12 minutes in a 350° oven.

MAKES about 25

These make any occasion a party but are especially fine with iced tea plus mint leaves on a summer afternoon in the garden. In winter, by an open fire, they go well with hot coffee.

JEAN'S NATURAL-GOOD COOKIES

¾ cup brown sugar
½ cup soft butter
1 tbsp molasses
1 tsp vanilla
1 egg
1 cup nuts (walnuts, pecans, or almonds),
　　measured, then grated
½ cup whole wheat flour, unsifted
¼ cup wheat germ
¼ cup oatmeal

Cream together the sugar and butter, then add molasses and vanilla, and beat well. Add egg, then add nuts, flour, wheat germ, and oatmeal, and beat well. Drop from a teaspoon onto a greased and floured cookie sheet. Bake 10 to 12 minutes in a 350° oven, or until browned.

MAKES about 2 dozen

You may add raisins or cut-up dates if you like, but why gild the lily? These cookies are naturally good eating as is.

DRUMLIN HILL SOUR CREAM COOKIES

1 cup butter or shortening
2 cups sugar
4 eggs
1 tsp baking soda dissolved in
1 cup commercial sour cream
3–3½ cups flour, sifted
    Grated rind of 1 orange
    Sugar as needed

Cream butter and 2 cups of sugar together. Add eggs singly. Beat well after each addition. Add the sour cream–soda mixture alternately with the flour. Add orange rind and sugar. Chill overnight, then turn on a floured board, roll out, and cut with a 3″ cutter. If the dough is too hard to work with, just drop by teaspoonfuls on a greased and floured cookie sheet (6 to a sheet). Sprinkle with the extra sugar and bake in a moderate oven (350°) until brown.

MAKES about 25

If you press down on the dough with a finger or the bottom of a glass dipped in sugar, Jean says, you will have more uniformly shaped cookies.

OATMEAL COOKIES

1	cup butter
1½	cups light brown sugar
1	egg, beaten
2	cups flour, sifted
1	tsp cinnamon
1	tsp soda and ⅛ tsp salt
4	tbsp cold water
1	cup rolled oats
1	cup raisins
½	cup nuts, coarsely chopped

Cream butter and sugar together, add the egg, and mix well. Add flour, cinnamon, soda, and salt. Mix well. Add water, then oats, raisins, and nuts. Drop from a teaspoon onto greased cookie sheets. Bake until brown in a 350° oven.

MAKES about 2 dozen

These cookies came from the kitchen of Mom Lovdal—Oscar's mother —and are a good addition to any cookie jar!

DRUMLIN HILL PEPPARKAKER

¼ cup butter
¾ sup sugar
½ cup sour cream
¼ cup caramel syrup (see below)
3 cups unsifted flour
1 tsp cloves
1 tsp ginger
1 tsp soda

Cream butter and sugar, add sour cream and syrup, then add sifted dry ingredients. If necessary add more flour so the dough is stiff. Chill overnight. Roll thin on a floured surface. Cut with cookie cutter. Bake at 375° about 7 minutes.

CARAMEL SYRUP

1 cup sugar
½ cup boiling water

Melt the sugar over low heat in a heavy skillet, stirring constantly to prevent burning. When sugar is melted and dark brown, remove from fire and stir while adding the boiling water (watch out as it bubbles). Continue stirring until smooth like maple sugar (put back on heat briefly if necessary).

MAKES about 2 dozen

These have a special flavor and store well.

TORCETTI—YEAST COOKIES

1 lb butter
1 lb Crisco
10 cups flour, sifted
1 cup warm milk
1 tbsp sugar
1 tbsp vanilla
2 yeast cakes
4 eggs, beaten
2 lbs 3-X confectioner's sugar

Cut the butter and Crisco into the flour until fine as cornmeal. Scald the milk, let cool to lukewarm, and combine with sugar and vanilla. Stir in the yeast until dissolved. Add yeast mix to flour mix. Beat in eggs. Add more flour if necessary and then knead slightly. Let rise until double in bulk (about 1 hour). Cover a board or counter with confectioner's sugar. Break off small pieces of dough and roll into a rope shape. Cut off 1½″ pieces. Place on greased cookie sheet and bake at 375° for about 12 to 15 minutes.

MAKES about 2 dozen

These are different and divine, as Jean says. The recipe can easily be cut in half, but since they freeze well and keep indefinitely, you can freeze them in cans, take out what is needed, and heat for 10 minutes or so. If you prefer them less sweet, use only 1 pound of confectioner's sugar. These cookies are perfect for Christmas giving. On a snowy Christmas Eve, Jean and Oscar are apt to drop in, Jean carrying an assortment of her cookies tied on a long scarlet ribbon with ever-greens at both ends. We hang it by the fireplace, and anyone who feels like having a cookie snips one off.

VIOLA'S SKILLET COFFEE CAKE

1½ cups sifted all-purpose flour
2   tsp baking powder
½   tsp baking soda
1   tsp salt
1   cup white sugar
2   eggs, lightly beaten
1   cup commercial sour cream
½   cup brown sugar, lightly packed
2   tbsp flour
2   tsp ground cinnamon
1   tsp vanilla
2   tbsp melted butter
½   cup coarsely chopped walnuts

Sift together the sifted flour, baking powder, baking soda, and salt. Combine and mix thoroughly white sugar, eggs, and sour cream. Heat electric skillet to 280° with cover on. When the light goes out, grease with salad oil (not olive oil). Add sifted dry ingredients to sour cream mixture and beat thoroughly. Spread batter evenly in bottom of the skillet. Cover and bake with the vent closed about 25 minutes, or until the top of the cake is dry.

Work together brown sugar, flour, cinnamon, vanilla, and butter and add nuts. Sprinkle this mixture over the top of the cake. Cover, turn dial off, let stand 10 minutes. Cut into squares.

SERVES 12

The temperature of the skillet may vary, depending on whether it has a glass or metal cover. Follow the directions for your own type. An electric skillet can be a life-saver if you have the oven full of ham or turkey or if the oven won't work! But I bet my mother could have made this recipe in an old cast-iron skillet!

COUNTRY GINGERBREAD

1   cup flour (unbleached if possible)
1   tsp soda
½   tsp ginger
¼   tsp cinnamon
¼   tsp cloves
¼   tsp salt
½   cup shortening
½   cup sugar
¼   cup molasses
1   egg
½   cup boiling water

Sift flour, measure, and sift again with soda, spices, and salt. Cream shortening until soft, then beat in sugar and molasses with a rotary beater until well blended. Add egg and beat well, then add flour mixture and mix well. Add boiling water and stir until blended. Bake in greased and floured pan in a moderate oven (350°) for 20 to 30 minutes, or until it draws away from the sides of the pan. You may use either an 8″-square pan or a 10″ x 13″ pan, depending on the thickness desired.

AND the number it will serve depends on how big a square you give each person.

When it comes to freshly baked gingerbread, use your own judgment. The Lovdals say it is good for breakfast too!

LETA'S CAKE

¾ cup cooking oil
¾ cup cold water
4   eggs, well beaten
1   pkg deluxe yellow cake mix
1   pkg instant lemon pudding (Jell-O)

Mix the oil, water, and eggs together, and add to the cake mix and pudding. Beat until smooth, then put in a large cake pan (14″ x 11″) and bake at 350° for 40 minutes. As soon as the cake comes from the oven, poke holes in it with a two-tined cooking fork. Then pour Orange Sauce by spoonfuls over the whole cake.

ORANGE SAUCE

2   cups powdered sugar—4X
2   tbsp cooking oil
2   tbsp water
⅓ cup orange juice

Beat all ingredients together until smooth.

SERVES 6–8

This serves a party and is nice to have on hand for holiday weekends. My friend Martha gave the recipe to me with a note saying that it has lots of calories, but then, so do most elegant things!

CONNIE'S POUND CAKE

1 pkg lemon Jell-O
¾ cup apricot nectar
¼ cup salad oil
4 eggs
1 pkg pound cake mix

Add the first 4 ingredients to the mix and beat well. Bake an hour at 325° in a loaf cake pan.

SERVES 4–6

This is a fine addition to a special afternoon tea, and we like it for dinner with cranberry sherbet after a simple one-dish main meal.

MARIE'S CHEESE CAKE

CRUST
Graham cracker crumbs

Use recipe on graham cracker box.

FILLING

2 3-oz pkgs cream cheese, at room temperature
½ cup sugar
4 large eggs, at room temperature
¼ cup flour (scant)
1 tsp vanilla

Beat the cheese and sugar, then add eggs one at a time. Sprinkle the flour over the cheese mixture and blend, adding vanilla. Pour into a 9″ springform pan. Bake in a moderate (350°) oven for 55 minutes. Remove from oven and increase the heat to 450° for 10 minutes. At end of 10-minute period, make the topping (next page).

TOPPING

1 pint sour cream
½ cup sugar
1 tsp lemon juice

Blend. Spread on the baked filling, and return to the 450° oven for 10 minutes. Remove cheese cake, cool on a rack, and refrigerate overnight.

MAKES 16 servings

Marie Schwalbe adds, "Some people like this for breakfast." This is because Barbara and I eat so much Ziegeuner Schnitzel and lentil salad for dinner, as well as the lentil soup, that we cannot eat another bite. We have coffee while Slim enjoys his dessert! Then Marie slips in with our cheese cake wrapped in foil, and we do have it for breakfast in the morning—and what a way to start the day!

BANANA CHIFFON CAKE

2¼ cups cake flour
1½ cups sugar
3 tsp baking powder
1 tsp salt
½ cup cooking or salad oil
5 medium-sized egg yolks, unbeaten
1 cup mashed ripe bananas (2 or 3)—use brown-flecked ones if possible possible
1 tbsp lemon juice
½ tsp cream of tartar
1 cup egg whites (7 or 8)

Sift flour, sugar, baking powder, and salt into a mixing bowl. Make a well in the bowl and add, one at a time, oil, egg yolks, bananas, and lemon juice. Beat until smooth. Add cream of tartar to egg whites, then beat in a large bowl until they form stiff peaks. Be sure you beat long enough! Then fold in the banana mixture tenderly, but do not stir—just fold. Pour into ungreased 10″ tube pan, 4″ deep. Bake in moderate oven (325°) about 1 hour and 5 minutes, or until a straw inserted in comes out clean. Turn pan upside-down *at once*, putting the tube part over a funnel or bottleneck so the pan is 1 inch above the table. Let the cake hang there until cold, then loosen from pan as much as possible with a spatula. Turn pan right side up, tap edge to loosen whole cake, and carefully remove from pan. Spread top and sides with frosting if you want it (we don't bother).

MAKES one 10″ tube cake with 16 or more servings

When bananas are in season and the children are tired of eating them "as is" and you have a lot getting riper by the minute, this makes a healthy dessert.

FRENCH CHOCOLATE CAKE

6 eggs
1 cup sugar
1 cup sifted flour
  Grated rind of 1 lemon
4 pieces dark chocolate
2 tbsp butter
  Shot glass of liqueur

Beat eggs and sugar well, then sift the flour over and add lemon rind. Add the chocolate pieces melted with butter and liqueur. Bake at 375° for 55 minutes in a regular square cake pan.

SERVES quite a few if you slice it thin. Or 6 can take care of it.

The size of the chocolate pieces can vary—I use about a handful, half to three quarters of a bar. The liqueur may be omitted but adds that French touch—Crème de menthe or Crème de cacao is good. This is a good thing to make when you just happen to have 6 extra eggs!

SOUR CREAM FROSTING

1½ cups semisweet chocolate pieces
¾   cup sour cream
    Dash of salt

Melt the chocolate over hot water. Remove from heat and stir in the sour cream and salt. Beat until creamy. Spread between layers or around the top and sides of your cake.

This is a rich, creamy, and elegant chocolate frosting—and so easy to make!

STRAWBERRY SHORTCAKE

2   cups flour
4   tsp baking powder
½   tsp salt
2   tsp sugar
⅓   cup butter
¾   cup milk
    Strawberries
    Heavy cream, ½ cup or so

Sift together flour, baking powder, salt, and sugar. Work in butter with your fingertips and add milk gradually. Toss and pat out on a floured board. Do not use a rolling pin. Pat the dough to fit a deep, round pie pan. Bake in a hot oven (425°) for about 15 minutes, or until brown on top. Remove from the oven and carefully split the shortcake in two. Butter both rounds.

Hull and slightly crush the berries while the shortcake is baking. Save some whole berries for garnish. Set the bowl of crushed berries near the stove to be slightly warmed. This brings out the flavor. Then pour the berries over the lower layer of shortcake, top with the second layer, and pour over more berries. The juice should run in a lovely rich stream down the sides. Top with whole berries and pour cream over the top.

SERVES 4–6

I am repeating this recipe since I get so many requests annually for it. It is the only real strawberry shortcake, and is a meal in itself, with the addition of hot coffee. What passes for strawberry shortcake is usually sponge cake with berries and isn't worth bothering with.

WALNUT TORTE

6	egg yolks
1¼	cups sugar
3½	cups finely grated walnuts
3	tsp almond extract
6	egg whites

Beat yolks until thick and tripled in volume. Gradually add the sugar, beating until very thick—about 10 minutes. Fold in the walnuts and extract. Beat egg whites until stiff. Fold ¼ of the whites into the yolk mixture, then fold in the remaining whites. Turn into a well-greased and floured 10″ x 13″ pan. Bake at 325° until the edges start to pull away from the sides of the pan. Cool. Turn out onto a rack. Cut into bars.

These bars may be cut in large squares and served with whipped cream for dessert or cut in small squares to serve with tea or coffee. They freeze well. They should be wrapped in foil after they are cool.

FRUITCAKE

1   cup diced citron
1   cup candied red and green cherries
½   cup cubed candied pineapple
½   cup diced candied lemon
1   pkg raisins, preferably white
1   can each walnuts, pecan halves, and slivered almonds
1   cup currants
½   cup sherry

Combine fruits, nuts, and sherry. Cover and let stand overnight at room temperature.

3   cups unsifted flour
½   tsp baking powder
½   tsp salt
2   tsp cinnamon
1   cup butter
2   cups sugar
1   tsp vanilla
6   eggs
⅓   cup sherry or brandy

Sift together first 4 ingredients. Beat butter, sugar, and vanilla until smooth (use a blender if you have one). Add the eggs one at a time, beating after each addition. When very light and fluffy, beat in the flour mixture. Add the batter to the fruit mixture; mix with a large wooden spoon. Turn into greased loaf pans (standard loaf pan). Bake 3 hours at 175°, or until a knife inserted in the center comes out clean. Cool completely in the pan on a wire rack. Then loosen the edge with a spatula, turn out of the pans.

Soak cheesecloth in sherry or brandy and wrap the cakes. Store in the refrigerator or in a tight container in a cool place. Resoak the cheesecloth when the cake begins to dry out, about once a week.

There are a good many excellent commercial fruitcakes on the market, but if you have time it is always fun to make your own. It keeps in-definitely and is very nice served in thin slices with hot coffee on a winter afternoon.

I prefer brandy to sherry for the extra touch, since sherry, even dry sherry, is a little sweet. Incidentally, you may vary the fruits accord-ing to your own taste. I have a friend who always uses pineapple. The basic idea of fruitcake is to use only enough dough to hold the fruit together.

WACKY CAKE

1½ cups unsifted flour
1   cup sugar
3   tbsp cocoa
1   tsp soda
½   tsp salt
1   tbsp vinegar
6   tbsp salad oil (or melted shortening)
1   tsp vanilla
1   cup cold water

Sift dry ingredients into an 8″ x 8″ x 2″ ungreased baking pan. Level it off and punch 3 holes into the mixture with the back of a spoon. Into one hole pour the vinegar, in another the shortening, and into the third, the vanilla. Pour the water over all and stir well with a fork. Bake 25 minutes at 350°.

SERVES 6–8

Margaret Bond sent me this as a time-saver; it keeps 4 or 5 days, which is an added dividend.

EASY PUFF PASTRY

1   cup butter
1¾   cups unbleached flour
½   cup commercial sour cream

Cut the butter into the flour with a pastry cutter or knife. Stir in sour cream until well blended. Wrap in foil and refrigerate overnight.

Roll out ⅛″ thick. Cut in desired shapes and sizes, and use the filling of your choice. For instance, fill center of squares with preserves and fold over or bring up the corners of the puffs. Or you may leave the pastry plain and use it for cocktail tidbits. Bake in a hot oven (400°) until delicately brown.

MAKES 10 squares or more, depending on how you cut them.

I always favor recipes made the day before and just finished off in time for the party. Jean often uses a prune and apricot stuffing, but almost any preserves are delectable.

HOT-WATER PASTRY

½   cup boiling water
½   lb lard
1   tsp salt
3   cups sifted flour

Add the lard to the boiling water with the salt. Mix thoroughly, then add the flour. Place in the refrigerator and let stand overnight. Roll out on a floured board in the morning.

I am repeating this recipe since so many people have told me they were never able to cope with pastry until they tried this. But it does not, I admit, do me personally any good: the smell of lard is too much for me, although I keep telling myself lard is the very best ingredient for flaky, rich pastry.

JAMES'S DE LUXE PUMPKIN PIE

2   cups canned pumpkin
3   eggs, separated
1   tsp cinnamon
½   tsp nutmeg
½   tsp ginger
½   cup brown sugar
½   cup white sugar
½   cup milk
1   tsp salt

Combine all ingredients except egg whites. Beat whites until stiff and fold into the mixture. Pour into pie shell and bake in a hot oven (400°) for about 50 minutes.

MAKES 1 9″ pie

James was for many years the cook and best friend of some Virginia friends of mine. He invented this recipe because most pumpkin pies, he thought, were on the heavy side and needed an iron-coated stomach. This is almost a chiffon pie but has more to it! Of course if you don't mind hard work, you can cook your own pumpkin, scrape out the pulp, and hash or put it in the blender to become smooth.

APPLE CREAM PIE

2½   cups chopped apples (Grimes Golden, if possible)
1   tbsp lemon juice
      Grated rind of ½ lemon
½   cup cream
3   tbsp flour, unsifted
⅔   cup white sugar
      Dash of salt

Mix all ingredients in a bowl. Fill uncooked pie crust with the mixture. Dot with butter and sprinkle nutmeg over the top. Bake 45 minutes or more in a 350° oven.

SERVES 4–6

This is a fine holiday dessert, worth saving room for.

MOCHA TART

4   egg yolks
1   cup sugar
1   cup sifted flour
2   tsp baking powder
1½ tsp mocha extract
4   egg whites

Cream egg yolks and sugar and blend in flour, baking powder, and mocha extract. Fold in stiffly beaten egg whites. Bake in 2 layers in greased cake pans at 350°.

FILLING

1 pint whipped cream
2 tbsp mocha extract
4 tbsp powdered sugar

Mix well and spread on both layers. Then pour over a mixture of the following:

2 cups confectioner's sugar
1 tbsp mocha extract
3 tbsp water (or enough to make it runny)

MOCHA EXTRACT

Mix together ¼ cup each of strong coffee and cocoa.

SERVES 4–6

You will have to live on grapefruit the next day.

CHOCOLATE MOUSSE WITH ORANGE RIND

1   pkg (6 oz) semisweet chocolate pieces
6   egg yolks
    Grated rind of 1 orange
⅓   cup sugar
6   egg whites
    Whipped cream

Melt chocolate in the top part of a double boiler over hot water. Beat egg yolks lightly and stir into chocolate. Heat several minutes, but do not let the water in the double boiler come to a boil. Add orange rind and sugar and cool slightly. Beat egg whites until stiff and fold into the chocolate mixture. Pour into individual serving dishes and chill for several hours. Serve with whipped cream.

SERVES 6

If you are dieting, leave out the whipped cream!

BARBARA'S CHOCOLATE MOUSSE

1   6-oz pkg semisweet chocolate bits
2   whole eggs
3   tbsp strong hot coffee
2   tbsp rum or brandy
¾   cup scalded milk

Mix all ingredients, using a blender if possible, and blend at high speed for 2 minutes. Pour into dessert cups and chill at least 6 hours.

SERVES 4

This recipe came from a Cape Cod cottage by the sea and is a perfect summer night dessert, especially when served on a patio within sound of the sea.

GINGER MOLD

1   tbsp unflavored gelatin dissolved in ¼ cup cold water
2   egg yolks
½   cup sugar
½   tsp salt
1   tbsp unflavored gelatin dissolved in ¼ cup cold water
1   tsp vanilla
¼   cup preserved ginger, cut fine
3   tbsp ginger syrup
1   tsp grated orange rind
½   pint cream, whipped stiff

Mix the milk, egg yolks, sugar, and salt in the top of your double boiler. Cook until thick. stirring constantly. Then add dissolved gelatin. Let cool. Add vanilla, ginger, syrup, and orange rind. Fold in the whipped cream. Pour into a ring mold and chill well. Unmold for serving and garnish with sprigs of fresh mint and slices of crystallized ginger, if you can get it.

SERVES 4–6

This is probably my favorite dessert, delicate and not too sweet.

PICKLES AND PRESERVES

SWEET CUCUMBER PICKLES

10	medium-sized cucumbers	2	tbsp whole black pepper
½	cup salt	1	stick cinnamon
2	qts water	¾	tsp mustard seed
1	qt cider vinegar	½	tsp whole cloves
1	cup sugar		

Wash cucumbers, drain and cover with brine made of the salt and water. Let stand for 24 hours. Drain. Add remaining ingredients and

259

heat to boiling point. Boil gently for 3 or 4 minutes. Pack pickles in hot sterilized jars and fill to overflowing with the syrup. Seal.

MAKES 1 quart

CUCUMBER OIL PICKLES

15	3″–4″ cucumbers sliced thin without paring
	Salt
¼	tsp alum dissolved in a little vinegar
1	cup olive oil
¼	lb whole black mustard seed
1½	tsp celery seed
	Sliced onions as desired
	Vinegar diluted with ⅓ water

Place cucumbers in a large jar in layers with salt between each layer and let stand overnight. In the morning rinse with cold water, place in a bowl, and pour over a mixture of the remaining ingredients except the vinegar and onions. (The alum—which makes the cucumbers crisper—may be omitted if you can't get it.)

Soak onion slices in ice water for 3 hours. Boil vinegar and water and chill. Then place cucumber mixture in sterilized Ball Mason jars and fill to overflowing with the vinegar and water. Add onion slices to the top of the jars, and seal jars.

MAKES about 5 quarts

This is a happy way to use up cucumbers if you have a vegetable garden, and they are good enough just to layer on fresh buttered bread and eat out of hand. Even if you haven't a garden, it is easy to buy cucumbers reasonably when they are overflowing the roadside markets.

BREAD-AND-BUTTER PICKLES

12   small or 6 large cucumbers, sliced (but not too thin)
6   onions, sliced
3   cups cider vinegar
1½   cups granulated sugar
1   tsp celery seed
1   tsp white mustard seed
1   tsp ginger
1   tsp turmeric
1   tsp pepper

Sprinkle cucumbers and onions sparingly with salt, add remaining ingredients, and let stand an hour or two. Boil all together in a heavy kettle for 10 minutes. Pour into sterilized jars and seal.

MAKES about 6 pints

This has been a family favorite for years. We like them spread on fresh warm slices of well-buttered bread for a snack! These pickles are also welcome served in a small bowl on a cocktail tray, with toothpicks for spearing.

WATERMELON PICKLES

2   qts watermelon rind
½   cup salt
2   qts water
2   cups vinegar
2   cups water
4   cups brown or white sugar
1   lemon, thinly sliced
1   stick cinnamon
1   tsp whole cloves
1   tsp whole allspice

Remove outer skin from watermelon rind and take out any pink portions. Cut into small pieces. Soak overnight in brine made of salt and the 2 quarts of water. Drain and wash with fresh water and drain again. Simmer in fresh water until tender. Make a syrup of the remaining ingredients and simmer for 5 minutes. Add rind and cook until clear. Pack into hot, sterilized jars, fill with syrup, and seal immediately.

MAKES 2 quarts

There is something about homemade watermelon pickles that is worth the effort, even though the supermarkets are full of commercially prepared ones. They also lend a helping hand to the budget and keep all that watermelon rind from going to waste!

JEAN'S RELISH

4 qts small green tomatoes
6 large onions
6 green peppers
6 red peppers
1 qt white vinegar
2 tbsp mustard seed
2 tbsp celery seed
2 tbsp turmeric
2 tbsp salt
2 lbs sugar (4 cups)

Grind together the first 4 ingredients and let drain. Then add the remaining ingredients and bring all to a boil. Cook 30 minutes. Pack in sterilized jars and seal.

MAKES 9 pints

Small tomatoes are best for this. And such a good way to use them!

CORN RELISH

18 ears sweet corn
1   small head cabbage, chopped fine
1   cup finely chopped celery
4   medium onions, chopped fine
2   green peppers, chopped fine
2   red peppers, chopped fine
1   qt cider vinegar
2   cups brown or white sugar
½   cup salt
3   tbsp dry mustard
2   tsp turmeric

Cook corn in boiling water for 2 minutes. Plunge into cold water. Drain and cut corn from cob. Add other vegetables and remaining ingredients and cook slowly for 30 minutes, stirring frequently. Pack in sterilized jars and seal.

MAKES 10–12 pints

And what a good way to preserve some of that summer goodness! Corn relish on the appetizer tray adds just the right touch, or serve it with cold sliced lamb or beef.

ETHEL'S SUPER HOT-DOG RELISH

Grind with the course blades of your grinder:

4 cups green tomatoes
4 cups onion
1 head cabbage
12 green peppers

Sprinkle ½ cup salt on the ground vegetables, mix, and let stand overnight, then rinse and drain. Combine the following:

6 cups brown sugar
1 tbsp celery seed
2 tbsp mustard seed
1½ tsp turmeric
4 cups cider vinegar
2 cups water

Pour over the vegetables and heat to boiling. Simmer for 3 minutes. Seal in sterilized jars.

MAKES about 4 quarts

You will find many uses for this relish and be glad you were patient enough to do all that grinding. And it is a lovely, economical way to get an extra dividend from garden or roadside vegetables. By the way, you may add a small jar of pimiento cut fine for a touch of extra color.

HULL'S HILL FARM CHILI SAUCE

24 ripe tomatoes
8 onions
3 peppers, red or green
3 tbsp salt
4 cups sugar
3 cups vinegar
3 tsp spices (pepper, cinnamon, and allspice)
½ tsp cloves

Skin the tomatoes if desired and cut into sixths. Chop or grind the onions and peppers and then put all ingredients into a large, heavy pot or preserving kettle. Boil until thick and pour into sterilized jars.

MAKES 9 or 10 pints

There is a special pleasure in making your own chili sauce. The good spicy smell in the kitchen is an extra dividend, and if you have your own garden vegetables or a good nearby vegetable stand, you will not have to bother with commercial chili sauce until all of your own is gone—and it will be soon enough.

TOMATO MUSTARD

18 large onions
36 large tomatoes
1 cup brown sugar
½ cup salt
1 qt cider vinegar (use ⅓ water to dilute)
¾ cup dry mustard
8 large sweet peppers

Peel onions, core and quarter tomatoes. Cook together until soft, then force through a sieve. Discard remaining pulp. Add brown sugar, salt, and all but a pint of the vinegar. Make a paste of the mustard and remaining pint of vinegar. Add to the first mixture and boil until it is the consistency of boiled custard. Grind the peppers and add just before turning off the heat. Pack in small, sterilized jars, and seal.

This is one of those secret recipes which I am finally sharing. It is good on almost anything except ice cream and is a Stillmeadow standby. We used to use vinegar or other small bottles, sterilized and capped with a bottle capper, but the jars are easier. Use your judgment about the amount of vinegar; add more if the mustard is too thick. And use only the best—and most expensive, alas—vinegar.

TOMATO HONEY

1 lb yellow pear tomatoes
  Boiling water to cover
1 lb sugar
2 lemons, thinly sliced
2 oz preserved ginger, cut in small pieces

Cover the tomatoes with boiling water and let stand until you can slip the skins off. Add the sugar and let stand overnight. In the morning, pour off the syrup and boil until fairly thick, then add tomatoes to the lemons and ginger. Cook until the tomatoes have a translucent look and the syrup is the consistency of honey. Cool, fill jelly glasses, seal, and store.

This is one of the best and most versatile of preserves. It is good on toasted English muffins, with cold roast duck or chicken, or on squares of hot cornbread.

GREEN TOMATO CHUTNEY

5	cups firm green tomatoes
1	seeded, diced lemon
1	clove garlic, minced
2¼	cups dark brown sugar
1½	cups seedless raisins
3	oz crystallized ginger, cut fine
1½	tsp salt
¼	tsp cayenne pepper
2	cups cider vinegar
2	minced red peppers, seeded

Simmer all ingredients until the tomatoes are tender but not too soupy. Put in sterile jars and seal. If you cannot get green tomatoes, use firm apples peeled and chopped fine. If you use apples, add about 1 cup of minced onion, since the apples may be too sweet.

MAKES 1½ quarts

This is one of the best standbys you can have in your kitchen. A spoonful on the plate with broiled lamb chops or baked chicken or roast beef just does something for the meal. If you cannot make it in your own kitchen, buy Major Grey's Chutney and keep it on your emergency shelf. But if you can make your own, you will find you love it, and of course it is easy on the budget! Also see the recipe for chutney and cream cheese spread in "Appetizers." It's the best!

PEAR CHUTNEY

3½ lbs ripe pears, peeled, cored, and chopped
3   cups seedless raisins
3   cups sugar
1   cup vinegar
    Grated rind of 2 oranges
1   tsp each cinnamon, cloves, and allspice
1   cup chopped pecans

Mix the first 4 ingredients, then add remaining ones except the nuts. Bring to a boil and simmer about 2 hours until thick. Stir nuts in and cook 2 minutes more. Put in sterilized jars and seal.

MAKES about 4 pints

This is a delicate and elegant version of chutney.

BAR-LE-DUC

3   qts ripe currants
6   cups sugar
½ cup honey

Stem the currants and put them in a large, heavy kettle. Crush gently but do not mash. Add sugar and bring to a boil. Boil gently for 5 minutes. Drizzle the honey over and boil 3 minutes more. Fill sterilized glasses and cover at once with paraffin.

YIELDS 8–10 half-pints

This is the perfect dessert served with toasted crackers and cream cheese. My cheese shop cuts cream cheese with a fine wire from a large rectangular block. It is not remotely like the foil-wrapped cream cheese in grocery stores. Try this if you have a nearby cheese shop.

APRICOT MARMALADE FROM THE LOVELYS

2 boxes (11 oz) dried apricots
3 oranges
4 lemons
1 small grapefruit
2 8-oz cans crushed, unsweetened pineapple

Soak apricots in cold water for an hour or so, then grind coarsely in a food chopper. Juice fresh fruits. Set skins aside. Mix together in large mixing bowl ground apricots, fruit juices, and pineapple. Measure by cupfuls into heavy aluminum saucepan or pot and add an equal amount of sugar. Mix well and let marinate, overnight if you like.

Put fruit skins in saucepan; add boiling water; simmer until soft but not mushy. Cool. Scrape out all pulp and pith from rind. Slice peel very thin. Add to rest of mixture. Bring mixture to boiling point very slowly and cook over low heat until clear. Fill jars and seal.

MAKES about 4 pints

After you try the above proportions once, adjust ingredients to your taste. We like things on the tart side rather than on the sweet, so I use only ⅔ of the amount of sugar and add the juice of an extra lemon plus extra peel, which I accumulate from breakfasts and save in a plastic bag in the refrigerator.

ROSE HIP JELLY

Gather wild or garden rose hips and remove stems. Wash in cold water. For each cup of hips add 2 cups of water. Boil for 15 minutes, then mash down and simmer for 10 more minutes. Set the mixture to rest for 24 hours or so in a glass or stainless steel bowl. Do not use aluminum.

Strain juice through a jelly bag or cheesecloth. Do not squeeze too hard. Then add 1 cup of apple juice to each 2 cups of juice and 1 box of pectin. Bring to a rolling boil, then add 4½ cups of sugar, stirring as you add. Boil about 7 minutes, or until the jelly drops in thickened sheets from a spoon. Remove from heat, skim, and pour in sterilized glasses or jars. Use melted paraffin to seal the jelly. Then cap and store in a cool place.

MAKES 6–10 jelly glasses full

Rose hips are the scarlet seedpods which develop on rosebushes in autumn after the roses have ceased blooming. They are best gathered in September before frost, and are a prime source of that vitamin C everyone is so addicted to nowadays.

MISCELLANEOUS

ASPARAGUS SANDWICH LUNCHEON SPECIAL

1 can cream of mushroom soup	6 slices bread, toasted
½ cup light cream	6 thin slices cooked ham
1 tsp lemon juice	2 lbs asparagus stalks, cooked
1 egg yolk, beaten	4 oz blue cheese

Mix the soup, cream, lemon juice, egg yolk, and heat until bubbly. Place the toast slices in a shallow baking pan. Cover each slice with a slice of ham and 4 asparagus tips. Pour the sauce over all. Top with blue cheese crumbled finely. Place under the broiler until the cheese melts. Dust with paprika.

SERVES 4–6

Be sure not to overcook the asparagus (See "Vegetables").

BITNER PLACE SCALLOPED PINEAPPLE CASSEROLE

½ cup butter
1   cup sugar
2   eggs
1   20-oz can crushed pineapple
3   cups bread cubes, packed firmly
1   cup marshmallow bits

Mix the first 3 ingredients, add the pineapple (undrained), bread cubes, and marshmallows. Bake in an uncovered casserole at 350° for 45 minutes to an hour, until browned and crusty on top.

SERVES 8

This is a fine companion to baked ham or broiled ham steaks or grilled pork chops. I like to add a little lemon juice.

BANANAS SINGAPORE

4 firm bananas
1½ tbsp butter or margarine, melted
3 cups Curry Sauce (see below)
1½ lbs fresh shrimp, cleaned and cooked (or frozen or
canned, allowing 6–10 shrimp per serving)
3 cups cooked rice

Peel bananas and place in baking dish. Brush well with butter, then pour half the sauce over. Bake in moderate oven (375°) for 15 to 18 minutes, until bananas are easily pierced with a fork. Meanwhile heat shrimp in the remaining sauce. Serve with bananas on a bed of hot rice.

SERVES 4–6

CURRY SAUCE

6 tbsp butter or margarine
6 tbsp flour
2 tsp curry powder
1 tsp salt
¼ tsp pepper
2½ cups chicken consommé

Melt butter in a saucepan. Add flour, curry powder, salt and pepper. Stir until smooth. Add consommé and cook slowly, stirring constantly, until sauce is smooth and creamy.

MAKES about 3 cups

If you wish, you may use 2 chicken bouillon cubes dissolved in 2½ cups of boiling water. In that case, omit the salt. We like more curry powder—test it by your own taste. This is a fine buffet one-dish meal and so pretty to look at!

SNOWED-IN CASSEROLE

1   onion, sliced
3   potatoes, sliced very thin
1   lb ground beef
¼   cup uncooked rice
½   cup chopped celery
2   cups red kidney beans
1   can (large size) cooked tomatoes blended with 3 cups water
     Salt, pepper, and paprika to taste

In a large buttered casserole, layer the first 6 ingredients, then pour the tomatoes on top and sprinkle with seasonings. Cover and bake at 325° for 2 hours. Add a bit of water if it gets too dry.

SERVES 4–6

Ann Hansen says this is a favorite of theirs when the snow is up to the windowsills.

TACO CASSEROLE

1 pkg (11 oz) corn chips, crushed
3 large or 4 medium-sized tomatoes, chopped
1 medium-sized onion, sliced
1 head lettuce, torn into bite-sized pieces
3 cans (1 lb each) chili con carne with
    beans (use the most expensive brand)
2 lbs sharp cheese, shredded

In 2 buttered 12-cup casseroles arrange the ingredients in the order given, in layers, dividing evenly. Bake 25 minutes in a 425° oven, or until hot and bubbly and the cheese is melted.

SERVES 10

The nice feature about this is you can MAKE IT AHEAD (These are favorite words in my cooking vocabulary!) We like it around Christmas as a change from the turkey, goose, ham, or whatever. Most guests take three helpings.

I am partial to one-dish meals during the holidays too, and all you need to serve with this is a fruit bowl and pots and pots of coffee.

SUMMER SUPPER SPECIAL

1 long loaf French bread
1 clove garlic, cut in half
1 cucumber, peeled and sliced
1 tomato, thinly sliced
4 pimientos, cut in half
8 black olives, pitted
1 small can anchovy fillets
  Olive oil
  White vinegar

Cut the bread in half lengthwise and rub the sides with garlic. Place the vegetables and anchovies neatly over the lower half and sprinkle lightly with oil and vinegar. Lay the top half over and press with a weight for 30 minutes or more. Slice for serving.

SERVES 6

This is fine picnic fare.

GNOCCHI

3   cups cold water
    Salt
1   cup white cornmeal
¾   cup grated Parmesan cheese
2   tsp dry mustard
1   egg, beaten
    Seasoned salt and pepper to taste
⅓   cup grated Parmesan cheese
⅓   cup melted butter
4   medium-sized tomatoes
2   pkgs brown-and-serve sausages
⅓   cup grated Parmesan cheese

Put the water and salt in a heavy saucepan and bring to a boil. Stir the cornmeal in slowly, stirring constantly. Cook until the cornmeal is creamy and thickened. It will begin to draw away from the sides of the kettle when it is done. Cover, reduce heat to low, and cook about 10 minutes more. Remove from heat and stir in first amount of cheese, mustard, egg, and seasonings. Turn into a 10″ x 6″ x 2″ baking dish, smoothing it with a wooden spoon.

Chill in the refrigerator until about 20 minutes before dinner, then cut into squares and arrange in the center of a large flat baking dish or metal skillet. Top with ⅓ cup of cheese and the melted butter. Start the broiler in the range. Cut the tomatoes in wedges and arrange at one end of the baking dish, sprinkle with seasonings and the remaining cheese. Broil 5 minutes, then add the sausages at the other end of the dish and broil until the sausages are brown and the cheese is bubbly.

SERVES 6

Garnish the dish with crisp watercress or parsley sprigs. This is a party dish and a favorite at Stillmeadow. I have no idea where it originated, but it came down in my family for generations, though, of course, there were no brown-and-serve sausages in those days. You used homemade sausages and partly cooked them ahead.

BASIC PIZZA

CRUST

1½ cups flour
½   tsp seasoned salt
1   tsp sugar
1   tbsp butter
½   cup hot water
½   pkg dry yeast

Mix flour, salt, and sugar in a bowl with a wooden spoon. Melt the butter in the hot water and let cool to lukewarm, then add yeast and let rest about 5 minutes. Then add to flour mixture and mix to a dough (it will be sticky). Dust your hands with flour and make a ball of the dough and set in an oiled bowl to rise for about 45 minutes, or until doubled in bulk. Meanwhile make the sauce:

PIZZA SAUCE

1   tbsp olive oil
1   onion, diced
1   clove garlic, minced
1⅓ cups Italian tomatoes, peeled
     and chopped but with juice
2   tbsp tomato paste
1   tsp oregano
1   tsp basil
½   bay leaf
½   tsp sugar
     Seasoned salt and pepper to taste

Sauté the onion in the oil until golden, add garlic and sauté about a minute, then add remaining ingredients and simmer at very low heat for about an hour, or until thick. Stir frequently. Remove bay leaf when finished.

TOPPING

½ lb Mozarella cheese
¼ lb Parmesan cheese

Grate cheeses and mix. Turn the dough onto a floured board and punch down, then pull the edges out into a circle, patting the dough into shape until it is about a foot in diameter. Transfer to buttered cookie sheet, pour the sauce over, sprinkle the cheeses over, and bake in a preheated oven at 450° for about 25 minutes. Serve very hot, cut in pie-shaped pieces.

SERVES 4

This is a basic pizza, and you may top it with whatever you like if you want to gild the lily (I don't). Pepperoni, anchovies, Italian sausage, mushrooms, green pepper, all are fine. Add them toward the last.

If you live near an Italian pizza place, you are better off popping in and getting it there. But real pizza is hard to come by in some areas, and making it is worth the effort once you admit how much you love pizza!

PAM'S PIZZA

1   cup boiling water
2   tbsp shortening
1   pkg dry yeast dissolved in a little warm water
3   cups flour
1½ tsp salt
    Pizza Sauce (see below)
    Parmesan cheese, grated
    Oregano
    Parsley flakes
    Sharp American cheese

Add shortening to boiling water and cool well, then add the yeast, and then the flour and salt. Mix well. Pam says she uses her hands toward the end and it helps. Spread the dough thinly on 3 medium-sized cookie sheets, well oiled. Let it rise for 1 hour in a warm place, then spread the warm sauce over the dough, and add grated Parmesan cheese. Sprinkle with oregano and parsley flakes, and top with slices of sharp American cheese (6 to 9 slices to a sheet). Bake in a hot oven (400°) for about 20 minutes, or until crisp and brown on the bottom. Cut in squares and put on racks to prevent it from steaming and getting soft.

PAM'S PIZZA SAUCE

1   medium onion, diced
2   cloves garlic, cut fine
⅓   cup olive oil
1   large can tomatoes
1   can tomato paste

Sauté onion and garlic in oil until tender, then add the tomatoes and the tomato paste. Let cook until bubbling, then turn heat off and let it cool slightly.

SERVES 4–6 (But real pizza people eat a whole one single-handed.)

Any leftover pizza may be wrapped in waxed paper and plastic bags and put in the freezer. Reheat in the electric frying pan for about 5 minutes.

LASAGNE

½   lb spaghetti
    Grated Parmesan cheese
    Cottage cheese
    Meat sauce
2   eggs
1   cup milk

Cook spaghetti until tender but not soft (al dente). Place a layer in a buttered baking dish. Sprinkle liberally with Parmesan cheese, then add a layer of cottage cheese, then the meat sauce (use your favorite —we like Escoffier). Continue to add layers until the dish is filled. Beat the eggs in the milk and pour over. Bake in a moderate oven for about 30 minutes.

SERVES 4–6

This is good eating for a weekend when friends happen by. Nice with spinach salad (see "Salads") or the traditional tossed greens. Italian dressing fits best.

BEVERAGES

ICED TEA

1   qt freshly drawn cold water
⅓   cup loose tea (Darjeeling or Constant
         Comment are our choice) or 15 teabags
1   qt cold water

Bring 1 quart of water to a rolling boil. Remove from heat and add tea at once. Stir, then cover and let stand 5 minutes. Stir again and strain into a pitcher holding 1 quart of cold water. Pour over ice cubes and garnish with mint leaves.

Refrigeration makes tea turn cloudy but does not damage the taste. Store leftover tea in glass or ceramic containers, not aluminum.

IRISH COFFEE

1 jigger Irish whiskey
1 or 2 tsp sugar
Fresh hot coffee

Heat the whiskey but do not let it boil; add sugar. Pour into coffee cup and fill the cup with the coffee. Stir until sugar dissolves.

SERVES 1

If you wish, float whipped cream on top of the cup.

CAFÉ ROYAL

1 orange
   Whole cloves
1 orange peel
1 lemon peel
2 cinnamon sticks
10 small sugar cubes
¾ cup brandy
4 cups fresh coffee

Stud the whole orange with cloves (18 or more). Slice orange and lemon peel thinly and put in a deep bowl with cinnamon sticks and sugar cubes. Heat brandy but do not boil. Pour over the orange and lemon peel and cinnamon and sugar. Ignite the brandy and ladle it over the bowl until the sugar melts. Now add 4 cups of fresh, hot coffee. Fill a ladle with ¼ cup of warm brandy, slide the whole orange in it and ignite. Lower ladle carefully into the bowl so the orange will float. Fill demitasse cups and serve hot.

SERVES 8, using demitasse cups

This is pretty fancy, but for an anniversary or a special holiday is worth it. It's even worth getting out great-grandmother's Wedgwood demitasse cups. We usually have our regular coffee in mugs.

SOUTH AMERICAN CHOCOLATE

1   oz chocolate
¼   cup sugar
     Dash of salt
1   cup boiling water
½   cup hot milk
½   cup hot cream
1½   cups fresh hot coffee
1   tsp vanilla
     Dash of cinnamon

Melt chocolate, sugar, and salt in the top of a double boiler over hot water. Add the boiling water and heat about 5 minutes more, then add the milk and cream and the coffee. Beat well and add the vanilla at the last. Dust with cinnamon.

SERVES 4

On a January day nothing is more welcome than this rich brew. While the mittens and boots dry in the back kitchen, we sip this by the open fire and decide winter isn't so bad after all!

SPANISH CHOCOLATE

2   cups light cream
2   cups milk
¼   tsp nutmeg or cinnamon
1   tbsp butter
8   oz semisweet chocolate (squares)
3   tbsp sugar
½   tsp salt

Combine all ingredients and heat, stirring with a wooden spoon, until chocolate melts. A double boiler is good for this. Remove from heat and beat with a rotary beater until it foams, then bring to a boil, stirring constantly. Remove from heat and beat again until frothy. Return to heat and beat, twice more.

SERVES 4

This sounds like a lot of beating, and it is. But it is worth it for those special evenings by the fire when you really have had enough tea and/or coffee during the day.

HOT BUTTERED RUM

¼ cup boiling water
1   tsp confectioner's sugar
¼ cup rum
1   tbsp butter

Heat the glass you will serve in or use a hot mug. Put the sugar in and add the remaining ingredients. Fill the glass or mug with boiling water and serve at once. You may sprinkle the top with nutmeg—I use cinnamon.

SERVES 1

This is supposed to have been the Pilgrims' brew and, when made in quantity, it was kept hot by dipping a hot iron in the bowl—the iron was called a loggerhead. Hot buttered rum was a remedy for everything from chills to snakebite and is still a help when the thermometer drops below zero.

TOM AND JERRY

4   egg whites
2   tbsp powdered sugar
4   egg yolks
½ jigger brandy
1   jigger light rum

Beat egg whites until stiff and gradually add the sugar. Beat in the yolks. Pour about 2 tablespoons of the mixture in each mug, then add brandy and rum. Fill the mug with hot water and stir.

SERVES 4

If you like nutmeg, you may sprinkle it on top.

HOLIDAY EGGNOG

12   eggs, separated
1½   cups fine granulated sugar
1   qt milk
1   qt heavy cream
1½   qts bourbon
1   pint cognac
2   tbsp dark rum
        Cinnamon

Beat the egg yolks until light and add sugar gradually, continuing to beat until the mixture is thick and light in color. Turn into a big bowl which you either have prechilled or place on a bed of ice. Now whip together the milk and cream, and very slowly add the bourbon and cognac, stirring (I use a wooden spoon). Beat the egg whites until stiff and fold in carefully. Sprinkle the top of the bowl with the dark rum and cinnamon.

MAKES 50 4-ounce servings

You may use nutmeg instead of cinnamon, but we prefer cinnamon. For an eggnog party on Christmas day, surround the bowl with holly or greens. If you do not have punch glasses, use small cups or mugs for serving.

FISH HOUSE PUNCH

1½ cups sugar
2   qts water
2   qts Bacardi rum
1   qt cognac
1   qt fresh lemon juice or 1 can frozen undiluted
1   wineglass peach brandy

Add 1 cup of water to the sugar and heat. Stir until sugar dissolves. Cool and put in large bowl. Add remaining water and liquids, stirring until well blended. Place a big chunk of ice in the punch bowl. Add the punch. Let stand 2 hours.

MAKES 50 cups, by the way

This is good for winter holiday sipping when the snow piles up against the windows and the open fire crackles.

WASSAIL

3   tart apples
2   qts cider
2   cups orange juice
⅔   cup lemon juice
2   sticks cinnamon
½   tsp whole cloves
½   tsp grated nutmeg
½   tsp ground allspice

Core the apples, cut in rounds, and bake. When they are fork-tender and browning, place them in a punch bowl. Bring the other ingredients to a boil and pour over the apples. Serve hot.

SERVES 10–15

On a below-zero winter day this is a welcome cup of cheer to sip while your boots thaw out in front of the open fire.

STILLMEADOW PUNCH

1 lb sugar, dissolved in boiling water
½ lb black tea, steeped (makes 4 qts)
2 cups lemon juice
3 cans chunk pineapple
½ dozen oranges, sliced

Mix the first 4 ingredients and pour into a large punch bowl. Float the orange slices on top.

MAKES enough punch for a party of 12–15

Taste as you go along, and if you do not like so much lemon juice, leave some out.

ODDS AND ENDS

I notice at a party when conversation takes a tailspin, one way to start it full speed ahead is to mention dieting. This interests both men and women for various reasons. There are those long, slim beautiful men who admit they can eat five meals a day but cannot gain an ounce. Some of us want to murder them. One of my favorite actors, Tony Randall, remarked on the Dick Cavett Show that he stuffs himself but just keeps losing weight, although he has nothing wrong with him!

There are leggy elegant women who may eat half a pound of chocolates when they are depressed (why are they ever?) but weigh exactly what they weighed in high school when they were the May Queen or something.

Then there are those of us who can merely walk by a savory dish of lasagne, take a good sniff—and gain half a pound. The battle of weight is always deadly. I belong in this group, although I was, as a child, so thin my father called me the starving Belgian. During high school and college, I ate anything I wanted to and came out all right. Even Wellesley fudge cake made no difference. But in my twenties, I began to look more and more like my parents and grandparents and the engravings of the early Mathers. We called it "stocky" in those days and accepted it as just a fact that I "took after" the family.

Much later, I began to go into half sizes. In spite of being a writer (25 calories an hour is all you spend for the hardest work you can do at the typewriter), I wasn't leading a sedentary life. At Stillmeadow, my beloved Jill and I painted, wallpapered, scraped floors, raised three extremely active children, several Irish setters, thirty-five cockers, and three cats. We also raised our own vegetables, had hens during one of those wars-to-end-war, canned and froze, made preserves, jellies, and pickles. Did our own corned beef too. We also did all of the cleaning in the 1690 farmhouse, all the washing, and the lawn mowing.

I was also writing countless short stories, a magazine column, and some books. When I was at the typewriter, Jill was cutting down dead apple trees for firewood or planting potatoes, or training the dogs in obedience work.

We both ate what I cooked, and we fed a houseful of guests on weekends. It was some years before I realized my college roommate could wear the same old clothes from our school days while I couldn't even get into my bathing suit! She simply never gained one solitary ounce and I was rounder than any robin.

I am going into this for the benefit of people like me. The two of us led the same kind of life and both felt that a nice way to rest was to go out in the woods and hike miles hunting arbutus and wild violets. But one stayed slim and one did not.

So when I began to do research of my own on weight control, I did not, I admit, pay much attention to the experts who maintain eating habits are the only major cause of poundage. Or to those who say a lack of exercise is the problem. I collected and read every book and magazine article available and then tried everything suggested. I still remember one summer when I would walk in the yard at the day's end, chewing a carrot and crying, while a houseful of happy people ate canapés around the open fire.

In the end, and it was a long end, I found out what worked for me. The diet the doctor gave me didn't work, partly because it was all in grams and you weighed and measured things. The high protein, the grapefruit, the cottage cheese—there are dozens of them, and all they did was throw me into such a profound depression I stopped dreaming of fiction and nonfiction, a depression that deepened when I stopped making any money to pay for reshingling the roof. It is highly possible to write when you are deeply sad, but not when you don't care about anything. For the basis of writing is a feverish urge to share your feelings, to communicate. Without it, you are just plain sunk!

Eventually I worked out my own personal diet, which took off forty-five pounds or more. Without ruining my life meanwhile.

So here is my recipe for dieting. Talk to the doctor about vitamins and supplements and arrange to go every four weeks to him to be weighed on one of those awful scales that weighs five or ten pounds more than your own bathroom one. The mere anticipation of that measuring keeps you firm. And the sweetest words you will ever hear are the doctor's when he says, "Well, you did all right this time. Five pounds less!"

Count the calories using a small pocket booklet such as most drugstores sell. Until you get used to it, look up and see how many calories there are in that helping of macaroni and cheese. Add them up each day and keep the overall count down to where you want it. If you are going to a party at night, subtract some calories from lunch. If you are due at an elegant luncheon, cut breakfast down to grapefruit and coffee.

One thing almost all experts agree on is the need for a hearty breakfast, but morning is one time I am not hungry and I simply skip the cereal and eggs and bacon and toast, etc. But if I am going on a long shopping spree, I eat a 6-minute egg with grapefruit and coffee.

Try to use up your calorie quota on vegetables like asparagus or tomatoes rather than beets. Broil everything you can broil. I myself do not like desserts or sweets, but if you need them, use fruits or gelatins. A compote of fresh fruit topped with one ripe strawberry is a delicious dessert. A lemon- or lime-gelatin whipped dessert is satisfying.

Check for loopholes in your diet. I found out early that tuna fish has a lot more calories than crab, for instance. I switched to crab. I love crab anyway! Meats also vary a great deal—lamb (fat removed) is better than roast beef. Chicken is a friend if you don't fry it.

Your calorie counter will tell you all you need to know. And if you keep the calories down, you lose weight.

Some people can be happy with dietetic foods, but I am not one of them. Raw vegetable salads are favorites with me, but I do not eat them with just a dash of lemon juice. I use Italian dressing, which I measure in a soup spoon and dribble over in a miserly fashion. I almost never eat butter, but when I broil scallops, I add lemon butter.

I feel dieting depends on your own way of life and your own preferences, and you should work it out to best suit you. If you must have sugar in coffee (I don't), add 18 calories every time you use a spoonful and subtract somewhere else.

Finally, the most important part of my diet is that I pamper myself about once a week and put that chart away. I found the lift in my spirits after one elegant dinner made the whole business easier. I talked to the doctor about this, and, surprisingly enough, he agreed with me. He said a vacation from a diet helps the morale.

I never changed my cooking while dieting. But when serving family and friends a delicious spaghetti, I simply cut my portion by one half or one third and had no seconds. This means you do not have to do double cooking, one kind for your slim family and friends and one kind for yourself. In some recipes you will find you can substitute part milk for cream, use more of those blessed mushrooms in casseroles and use pan juices with fat skimmed off rather than a rich happy gravy. You will serve more tomatoes and fewer green peas. You will not give up potatoes but will save the scalloped ones for your pamper days and settle for a small baked potato with your broiled lamb steak. When you serve nice warm apple pie, cut a piece for yourself no wider than a knifeblade.

When you have lost ten pounds you may do as I did. I went out with Barbara Lovely and had a pizza, and it was marvelous! (Your quota for the day, said the doctor.)

I think one reason my own diet works is that if you start to gain, you merely cut some calories. Also you may buy an expensive dress in the size you want to be, and reduce into it!

As far as diet pills and reducing gadgets are concerned, I have never tried any and never expect to. I read the ads and think dreamily about melting away the pounds with rubber straitjackets or electric massagers or by simply swallowing a few pills daily, but I am never really tempted. My own reducing plan is safe and sane.

Here are a few extra tips I have found helpful. Most experts say firmly, NO SNACKS. However, if I go to bed full of nothing but emptiness I do not sleep. I have a lovely snack plate around midnight. A fat ripe pear cut in thin slices. Four or five English water crackers (no fat). A little wafer-slim spreading of cheese. Or an apple or a few grapes. I call it my survival kit.

In midafternoon, if I am working long hours, I have tea with lemon or a mug of bouillon. Or black coffee (but I try not to drink too much coffee except at meals). I always have one teaspoon of butter somewhere along the line and a teaspoon of currant jelly to provide some sweet. The jelly goes on crackers or dry toast.

I keep Sahara bread on hand (a flat, thin Syrian circular loaf with no fat in it, available at most supermarkets) and split it and run it under the broiler with my teaspoon of butter brushed over it. We all need some bread, I think, and homemade breads are full of nourishment. I have a slice when the family has it, but slice my own thin, cutting the calories in half!

Omitting potatoes and bread means you miss something needed for a balanced diet, so at least once or twice a week, I have that baked potato with a broiled lamb steak and a dish of asparagus for dinner.

Celery, carrots, crisp lettuce, and sliced ripe tomatoes are a dieter's first aid. I put them in ice water (except the tomatoes) until they are all crunchy and good. Then I keep a bowl on the trestle table to dip into. Sprinkling chopped chives on the tomato slices makes them taste better.

I find beef or lamb stew very useful. I make it ahead of time and let the fat rise and skim it off. For hamburgers, I use lean ground beef and broil it. It costs more than the packaged kind in supermarkets but has almost no fat.

You will find your own ways to keep the calorie count down once you start.

Finally, when I go to parties, I eat one or two of those elegant puff canapés instead of the whole tray I could so easily devour. Almost every hostess nowadays serves a bowl of raw vegetables, and I have those for seconds.

If I am going to a very special festivity when I know dinner will be very late, I have a cup of tea or bouillon with two or three crackers around five o'clock. For when you are on a diet, you need your sustenance at the same time daily. If you don't get it, you either have a headache or a pain in your middle, or you eat too much when you finally sit down at the table.

When the day comes that you have to give away all of your clothes because they hang on you like potato sacks, you will know it is worth it! Then you have only to check the scales often enough to be sure the pounds do not slip back. And you can celebrate with two helpings of spaghetti! Or a nice helping of chocolate mousse!

Index

NOTES

NOTES

NOTES

NOTES

NOTES

NOTES

NOTES

NOTES